Narrative Conventions
of Truth
in the Middle Ages

JEANETTE M.A. BEER

Narrative Conventions
of Truth
in the Middle Ages

LIBRAIRIE DROZ S.A.
11, rue Massot
GENÈVE
1981

To R.E.D., SJ

Introduction

The existence of a common heritage of formulae and themes among European vernacular and Latin authors of the Middle Ages was demonstrated by E.R. Curtius in *Europäische Literatur und lateinisches Mittelalter*. After the appearance of that influential work in 1948, the search for *topoi* became for a time one of the more absorbing interests of medieval scholarship. The identification of recognizable conventions did not always lead to profound analysis of their usage. Indeed, the medieval use of *topoi* was often viewed as misuse or even abuse of « the classical heritage ». But a medieval imitator was not a slave of his rhetorical masters, whom he parodied as readily as he parroted. This book attempts to show that the seeming misuse of a convention, if consistent, was not accidental — continuing incongruity between conventional content and author's intent could become a convention in itself.

The example chosen for study was the truth assertion, because it had received little or no attention, and because the dogmatic statement HERE-IS-TRUTH had considerable importance in any narrative text. The assertion could be lengthy or brief in form. Einhard in his prologue to the *Vita Caroli Magni Imperatoris* asserted the truth of his biography by «ab hujuscemodi scriptione non existimavi temperandum, quando mihi conscius eram nullum ea veracius quam me scribere posse, quibus ipse interfui quaeque praesens oculata, ut dicunt, fide cognovi et utrum ab alio scriberentur necne liquido scire non potui ». Marie de France's « les contes ke jo sai verrais » in the opening lines of the lay « Guigemar » made the same truth claim in a single word without explanation. Despite all dissimilarities, Einhard and

Marie de France had this literary device in common. And like the brevity-formula (which so often appeared in contexts of interminable enumeration), the assertion of truth was made in the most paradoxical circumstances.

Before examining these circumstances it will be helpful to summarize the most important medieval assumptions about truth. Isidore of Seville's *Etymologiae* is their best compendium. Isidore's etymology of « verus » was informative by its very lack of information : « verus, a veritate ; hinc et verax. Maior est veritas quam verus, quia non veritas a vero, sed verus a veritate descendit » (I, x, 275-6). Truth being truth and thus, presumably, recognizable from falsehood, it needed definition merely by an etymology and not by its properties. Isidore posited for truth a hierarchy of values by word-class, in which « true » was subordinate to «truth » because the adjective « verus » derived from, and was chronologically subordinate to, the substantive «veritas ». Such theorizing had metaphysical implications — it extolled pure abstraction (« veritas ») over the attribute derived therefrom (« verus »). There were practical effects also. Truth and facts were polarized, with preference for the former over the latter in contexts of apparent conflict.

Truth separated history (« res verae quae factae sunt ») from fable (« fabulae vero sunt quae nec factae sunt nec fieri possunt ») (I, xliv, 5). History was the narration of events. It was so named « ἀπὸ τοῦ ἱστορεῖν » which Isidore (incorrectly) translated as seeing (« videre ») and learning («cognoscere») (I, xli, 1). The eye-witnessing of events was the best source and the best guarantee of historical truth, for what was seen was related without lies : « quae enim videntur, sine mendacio proferuntur » (*ibid.*). Isidore's assertion of the reliability of eye-witness history ignored such complicating factors as personality, background, and political motive. It subordinated style to content, for the « res gesta » and not the manner of its « narratio » now defined history. Thus the genre that Quintilian had once regarded as most akin to poetry and as most deserving of stylistic elaboration was now redefined according to logical rather than aesthetic criteria. History now dealt with happenings. History was also a didactic lesson for humanity, and for this even heathen history might serve. The « res verae » of antiquity could be sifted by the moderns for the purpose of demonstrating truth : « veritas ».

The above assumptions about truth can be assembled into the following recipe : Latin (i.e.) pagan authors were medieval authorities ; they were without the « truth » ; the Christian should not read the lies of pagan poetry ; pagan histories that dealt with useful subjects were not harmful ; the post-Classical Christian ages were superior to all past ages ; history — a part of grammar — committed what was worthy of memory to letters ; an eye-witness testimony of events guaranteed truth ; the facts were subordinate to the « truth ».

The ingredients were disparate, but it was not their disparateness that made the truth assertions suspect. It would seem rather that a tradition of manipulation gradually became associated with such assertions, so that Guillaume de Machaut eventually could name his monumental hoax *Le Livre du Voir-dit* from the convention. Further research upon other conventions should reveal whether they too could be used to contrary purpose.

Chapter One

Truth and the Authorities

Guillaume de Poitiers reflected all of Isidore of Seville's assumptions about truth in the *Gesta Guillelmi ducis Normannorum et regis Anglorum*[1] for which he made frequent truth claims. Ostensibly it told the truth about a man of truth in a truthful medium — prose. Guillaume's truth-proposition might be formulated as follows : truth is superior to falsehood ; the *Gesta Guillelmi* relates the true facts of William's life, which was devoted to truth ; *ergo*, the *Gesta Guillelmi* surpasses all the heroic writings of antiquity, since they embellished the truth and cultivated lies. « Scriptor Thebaidos vel AEneidos, qui libris in ipsis poetica lege de magnis majora canunt, ex actibus hujus viri aeque magnum, plus dignum conficerent opus vera canendo », II, 22.

This truth assertion disguised a paradox : although the artistic supremacy of the *auctores* was their weakness in Guillaume's view, it was the *auctores* that provided Guillaume with his structural and stylistic models. Guillaume's training in humane letters at the Poitiers schools was his literary trademark : « Pictavinus autem dictus est, quia Pic-

[1] Guillaume de Poitiers, *Gesta Guillelmi ducis Normannorum et regis Anglorum*, ed. R. Foreville (Paris, 1952). The text as it survives lacks a prologue, beginning in mid-sentence with the death of Cnut (1035) and ending in mid-sentence with the death of Copsige, Earl of Northumbria (1067).

tavis fonte philosophico ubertim imbutus est. »[2] Agamemnon, Achilles, Hector, Turnus, Pompey, Mithridates, Marius, Jugurtha, Pyrrhus, Augustus, Cicero, and Plato were among the many references to classical literature in the *Gesta Guillelmi*, and Suetonius' *Vitae* was a visible influence upon its structure.

Guillaume aimed to prove the superiority of present over past on the evidence of his biography of a Christian conqueror-duke. William was nevertheless measured against antiquity on antiquity's terms. Agamemnon, king of Argos, had waged ten years of siege to win one city, but William had subjugated all England in a day : « Argivorum rex Agamemnon habens in auxilio multos duces atque reges, unicam urbem Priami dolo vix evertit obsidionis anno decimo ... Subegit autem urbes Anglorum cunctas dux Guillelmus copiis Normanniae uno die ab hora tertia in vesperum, non multo extrinsecus adjutorio », II, 26. Tydeus had defended himself single-handed against fifty attackers, but William had not feared to fight one thousand : « Tydeus adversum insidiatos quinquaginta rupis petivit opem : Guillelmus par, haud inferior loco, solus non extimuit mille », II, 22. Julius Caesar had been rash of temperament, and had trusted excessively to Fortune. William had acted prudently at all times, and had owed his success to wisdom rather than to chance : « Si Romani illius, et nostri principis acta attentius perspexeris, illum temerarium atque fortunae nimis confidentem, hunc omnino providum hominem, qui magis optimo consilio quam casu res bene gesserit, recte dices », II, 40.

It had been the property of classical poetry to embellish — fiction was its product. It was the property of medieval prose to state facts simply — truth would be its product. Guillaume's truth claim here was essentially a denigration of his authorities, and his « meager prose » (II, 22) was the

---

[2] Orderic Vital, *Historia ecclesiastica*, ed. A. Le Prévost and L. Delisle (Paris, 1838-55), IV, ii, p. 217.

outward sign of inner grace. Poets amplified. Vergil's pen was mightier than Aeneas' sword. Guillaume's history would be justified by fact alone : « Parturire suo pectore bella quae calamo ederentur, poetis licebat, atque amplificare utcumque cognita per campos figmentorum divagando. Nos ducem sive regem, cui nunquam impure quid fuit pulchrum, pure laudabimus ; nusquam a veritatis limite passu uno delirantes », I, 20.

Paradox can again be found in the descriptions of the author's method, and Guillaume's assertions of truth are, by definition, assertions of partiality, because his « truth » was eulogistic — « laudabimus ». Although Guillaume compares favorably with contemporary Norman propagandists[3] for the reliability of the facts presented,[4] those facts have been adapted to his purpose. Eulogy implies authorial selectivity in dealing with the material. Facts that are « appropriate (only) in volumes of annals » must be omitted in favor of the « praestantissima » : « Praeterea quantulum in dicendo facultatis habemus, ad dicendum praestantissima omnium id reservamus », I, 20.

Amplification was used to enhance the most outstanding exploits so that the Gesta Guillelmi would provide an illustrious example for posterity, for example, William's donations (II, 31) and the loyal alliance of Copsige (II, 48). Other passages which have been demonstrably amplified ad praeconium are the description of the young duke William at the time of his alliance with Henry of France (I, 11-12), the

[3] For example, Guillaume de Jumièges, Gesta Normannorum ducum, ed. J. Marx (Rouen and Paris, 1914). The controversy concerning possible influence of the Gesta Normannorum ducum upon the Gesta Guillelmi is not resolved. There are some stylistic resemblances, and no major factual discrepancies. Minor differences in chronology and other miscellaneous areas are sufficiently frequent, however, to suggest that Guillaume de Poitiers's main source was consistently his own experience in preference to that of another.

[4] Because of the neglect of the Gesta Guillelmi by medieval scholars to date, a summary is given in Appendix One.

Ambrières victory over Geoffrey Martel (I, 33), the virtues of Marguerite, the intended bride of William's son, Robert (I, 39), the qualities of William (I, 47-59), the qualities of William's supporter, pope Alexander (II, 3), William's conquest (II, 26), the archbishop Ealdred of York, who crowned William (II, 30), and William again (II, 32).

Apostrophe was employed for a more dramatic expansion of the facts or, in some cases, for their abridgement, as in the following reproach to England deploring (but not describing) her lukewarm acceptance of William : «Diligeres, ac maximi haberes eum et tu, Anglica terra, totamque te ejus pedibus laeta prosterneres, si abesset imprudentia atque iniquitas tua, quo meliore consilio dijudicare posses in qualis viri potestatem deveneris... » (II,32). Guillaume's apostrophizing was frequently condemnatory. The vituperative denigration of William's enemies contributed directly to the laudatory process, however, since it provided thematic lines of development for the eulogy of William : « Paucis igitur te affabimur Heralde. Qua mente post haec Guillelmo haereditatem auferre, bellum inferre, ausus es, cuique te gentemque tuam sacrosancto jurejurando subjecisti tua et lingua et manu ? » (I, 46), (see also I, 4 and II, 25).

The author's favor or disfavor for political figures was, by his own admission, dependent upon more than the facts of a given historical situation. In the case of Eustace of Boulogne, for example, his treacherous abandonment of William and his support of Kent were glossed over. Because he was now numbered among William's close associates, the author spared him the vituperation he deserved: «Sed parcendum sentimus personae multifariam illustri, comiti nominato, qui reconciliatus nunc in proximis regis honoratur » (II, 47). Obviously a current political situation could work retroactively upon the « vera » of the Gesta Guillelmi.

Other stylistic devices which contributed to Guillaume's purpose were digression (on the personal qualities of one of William's family appointments, bishop Hugh of Lisieux, I, 58), exclamatory pathos or mock pathos (at the surrender of

Arques, I, 27), hyperbole (« Guillelmus, gloriosissimus dux », I, 4), epic periphrasis (« ductor terribilis », I, 45), sententious didacticism (« Quod humanae linguae ad malevolentiam quam ad benevolentiam laudandam sint promptiores, novimus », I, 36), emotive language (« vix enim hujus inimici odium et rabiem Normanniae tellus penitus contusa vel excisa satiaret », I, 34), and expansion by oration (William's harangue to his army, II, 15).

The above techniques did not necessarily alter the facts. Eulogy *was* detrimental, however, when it imposed particular lines of development upon the biography. The subject-matter of the *Gesta Guillelmi* may be viewed overall as an illustrative argument to justify William's conquest and his legitimacy as an English king, his brutality in achieving that end, and his nepotism after he had achieved it.

The right of a Norman duke to rule England by virtue of conquest was the underlying thesis of the *Gesta Guillelmi*. It was addressed explicitly many times (for example, I, 13 ; 14 ; 41 ; 42 ; II, 1 ; 3 ; 12 and 30). A more indirect approach was the somewhat unsuitable exploitation of Graeco-Roman abomination of « tyranny » for the whitewashing of a Norman war-lord. The loaded word « tyrannus » denigrated William's enemy Geoffrey Martel when he sent aid to Domfort (I, 18) and when he supported Geoffrey of Mayenne against William at Ambrières (I, 32 twice in the same section). « Tyrannus » was used also of all who opposed William at the Battle of Hastings (« tametsi tyrannum occidere sit pulchrum, fama gloriosum beneficio gratum » , II, 25). Among those, William's arch-rival was singled out, « abominandum tyrannum », II, 32.

William's acts of brutality also were justified by classical authority when the Caesarean image was imposed upon the narrative. « Julium Caesarem, vel bellandi peritiorem aliquem, si fuerit peritior, exercitus Romani ducem, ex mille nationibus coacti olim dum Roma florentissima mille provinciis imperitasset, hujus agminis immanitate terreri potuisse affirmaris », I, 30 (see also II, 32 ; 39 ; 40). Whole passages (for example, I, 30) were modelled stylistically upon the *Bellum Gallicum*, and individual features were borrowed from the same work for similar purpose. The antiphrasis by which Caesar had ironically labelled his brutality as « clementia » was used occasionally in the *Gesta Guillelmi* for William's acts of « generosity » (I, 19 ; 26 ; 28 ; 38). The narrator's labelling of the English as « barbari » repeated Caesar's term for his opponents in Britain, and the author's espousal of William's cause was indicated by his mimicking of Caesar's « nos » and « nostri » (II, 17 and *passim*). Even Guillaume's all-pervasive Norman propaganda followed Roman precedent.

William's nepotism was usually justified by eulogy. Narration of his ecclesiastical appointments was interrupted by digressions concerning the personal qualities of those family members who had been exalted to the bishopric (Hugh of Lisieux, Odo of Bayeux, and John of Avranches, « quorum in electione penes judicium ejus probitas ipsorum valuit, non altitudo natalium proximorum ipsi », I, 56). When ducal selectivity might be called partiality, authorial selectivity arranged the facts.

Another controversial issue was William's marriage to Mathilda, daughter of Baldwin V of Flanders, and again the facts were either omitted or adapted. The marriage was described as William's obedient response to his prudent councillors' urgings : « Reges de longinquo suas unice charas filias huic marito voluntarie locarent, at affines habere quos confines potissimum placuit, multae rationis gravitate id persuadente », I, 21. The fact that the marriage constituted insubordination to a papal prohibition was not mentioned. Instead, the political suitability of the match was argued through a eulogy of Baldwin's dynasty. That eulogy ended in the inexpressibility-topos that no amplification could do justice to the marquis' achievements and temperament : « Marchio hic fascibus ac titulis longe amplior quam strictim sit explicabile, natam suam nobis acceptissimam dominam in Pontivo ipse praesentavit soceris generoque digne adductam », I, 22. William's choice of marriage partner was not discussed again, although there was a brief mention of Mathilda's success in ruling Normandy during William's absence : « Optime quidem egerat in gubernaculo domina nostra Matildis, jam nomine divulgato regina etsi nondum coronata », II, 43. The final outcome of the marriage had obviously justified William's religious disobedience, despite the controversy and excommunication.

It should by now be obvious that all of Guillaume's assertions concerning the truth of the *Gesta Guillelmi* must be tempered by his statement of his eulogistic intent. His juxtaposition of « quam verissime tradere » and « cunctis placere » was significant : « Quapropter nos operae pretium arbitramur quam verissime tradere, quatinus Guillelmus hic (quem scripto propagamus, quem tam futuris quam praesentibus, in nullo displicere, imo cunctis placere optamus), Cenomanico principatu, quemadmodum regno Anglico, non solum forti manu potitus fuerit, sed et justitiae legibus potiri debuerit », I, 36.

When Guillaume used truth assertions for particular aspects of his work, the material they introduced was no less partial and selective. The causes of French resentment against the Normans were guaranteed to be a true and full disclosure of the facts : « Inimicitiae causas veraciter explanamus ac pleniter», I, 29. The explanation included, however, the attribution of unverifiable and violently emotive sentiments to the enemies of the Normans : « Anxie tumebat in eorum malivolis mentibus vulnus praecipue invidum, quod recenter sauciavit ... Acerbe inflammabat eos memoria eventus Andegavorum comitis Gaufredi ... »

Although the above « explanation » was followed by a more dispassionate treatment of the supposed threat that William presented to his neighbors (by his alliance with the Emperor Henry III, the military support he commanded, and his rejection of Normandy's subordinate stance towards France), the exposition remained a pro-Norman reconstruction of enemy passions, which ended appropriately in an impassioned espousal of regional loyalties :

> Nimirum concipit pavorem aliquantum terra nostra. Ecclesiae metuunt inquietanda fore otia sanctae religionis, stipendia sua ex libidine armatorum diripienda, quamvis orationum praesidio certantes confidant. Plebs urbana et agrestis necnon quicunque imbellis et minus firmus, solliciti sunt ac trepidi : timent sibi, uxoribus, liberis, rebus suis, cum adeo gravem hostem timoris modo ampliorem quam sit metiuntur. At cum reminiscuntur quem habeant propugnatorem, quam luctuosas patriae calamitates adhuc adolescens, vel puer potius, magno consilio, maximaque virtute sustulerit, spe timorem leniunt, afflictionem fiducia consolantur (I, 30).

Similar rhetoric embellished William's seizure of Maine, the controversial aspects of which were only intimated by the author's cryptic *sententia* that the most virtuous actions of the great are blamed when they are inaccurately reported : « Unde nonnunquam fieri constat, quatinus decora regum, sive ducum, sive cujuscunque optimi, cum non vere traduntur, apud aetatem posteram censura bonorum damnentur », I, 36. That imputation of untruth to *other* historians introduced an assertion of Guillaume's own truth-by-eulogy (see above, p. 19). If Guillaume had established that William's claim to Maine was legitimate, then Walter of Vexin became a « tyrant » when he inherited Maine. Furthermore, William's subsequent harassment of Maine, and of any other region under « tyranny », was justifiable and necessary behavior to recover what belonged to him.

Predictably succession — this time to the English throne — was also the occasion for an authorial assertion of truth. « As the most truthful and outstandingly honest witnesses have testified » (« sicut veracissimi multaque honestate praeclarissimi homines recitavere », I, 42), Earl Harold swore an oath of fealty to William concerning the English succession. Since the oath included specific details of homage, fealty, and investiture, William's « invasion » of England after Edward's death was actually not invasion, but rather the collection of what was already his. « Invasion » was again revealed to be a misnomer by the author's guarantee that all of William's wars were just. « Nec vere dictum unquam erit suscepisse eum bellum quod justitia vacaret », I, 48.

The legitimacy of William's cause was assured also by his defence of the true faith, « sincera fide tenens quod vera doctrina praeceperat: panem et vinum quae altari superponuntur, consecrata sacerdotis lingua et manu sancto canone, redemptoris veram esse carnem et verum esse sanguinem », I, 49. He was given political support for that cause by a pope whose life was devoted to truth : « Neque sui cursus limitem sol immutabilius natura, quam per veritatis ille directum tendebat vita », II, 3.

As for William's own probity, if anyone had been able to scrutinize all his acts from childhood on, that person would « truly » have affirmed that William never deviated once from any obligation of alliance or friendship : « Cum ab illa ad aetatem hanc, vel si majus a pueritia pernoveris ejus actus, tute, sicuti vere potes, affirmabis per eum nunquam societatis jus aut amicitiae fuisse violatum », I, 13. This truth assertion was more than usually ineffectual, since it was guaranteed by a hypothetical future observer of William's life from childhood to the grave ! The majority of Guillaume's truth claims relied, however, upon his own authority or experience. The bounty that William lavishly bestowed from English gains upon many Norman churches was « truly » his : « Rex vero Guillelmus nunquam nisi bonitate sinceram famam sibi comparavit, donans vere sua », II, 42. As for the wealth of his feast-table, the author might with truth relate incredible things : « Item vasa argentea sive aurea admirabantur, quorum de numero vel decore vere narrari possent incredibilia », II, 44.

A juxtaposition of truth to the incredible was not unusual in the *Gesta Guillelmi*, since paradoxical couplings accompanied the author's truth assertions in every context. Each time truth was guaranteed, underlying paradox or controversy could be found. Not least of these paradoxes was the conception of the whole work as an embodiment of modern truth. « Xerxem fabulatur illa Seston et Abidon ponto disjunctas urbes navium ponte conjunxisse. Guillelmum nos revera propagamus, uno clavo suae potestatis Normannici soli et Anglici amplitudinem copulavisse », II, 7. The assertion declared war and admitted dependence upon classical models. Truth was judged as if it were fable. In this measurement of William against antiquity it was antiquity that Guillaume found wanting. His criteria were curiously scientific in view of the literary contexts involved : the time required for siege, the number of the opposing enemy, the behavior of the conqueror after conquest, or the degree of chance in the conqueror's strategy. But by whatever criteria they were judged, the *auctores* dominated Guillaume's historical truth. The « vera » of an eleventh-century general had been assessed in the light of classical fiction, and the author's rejection of his models remained his acceptance of them.

Truth in the *Gesta Guillelmi* was a complex combination of eulogy and didacticism, eye-witness detail and omission, contemporary documentation and classical illustration, Norman politics and universal truth, « meager prose » and rhetorical embellishment. In this complex interaction between a medieval author and his authorities, Guillaume revealed the influence of the old by asserting the uniqueness of the new. His assertions of truth were indicators of conflict.

Chapter Two

Truth and the Eye-Witness

Throughout the Middle Ages classical authorities continued to serve as models for the genre that was defined by its adherence to truth : history. But formal imitation of the ancients was neither a sufficient nor a necessary condition for history's production. History was a narration of events, «narratio rei gestae» (*Etymologiae*, I, xli, 1). Its main function was the preservation in writing of whatever was worthy of posterity's attention : « quidquid dignum memoria est litteris mandatur. Historiae autem ideo monumenta dicuntur, eo quod memoriam tribuant rerum gestarum » (*ibid.*). Its derivation from « videre » and « cognoscere » defined it as an amalgam of seeing and knowing (see above, p. 10). Isidore's definition of history contained also the bold and influential non-sequitur that the eye-witnessing of events was the best guarantee *not only* of the accuracy of the historical information *but also* of its presentation. « Quae enim videntur, sine mendacio proferuntur » (*ibid.*). Truth came from the eyewitness.

Isidore's belief in the reliability of a history that had been personally experienced by the historian relegated form to a secondary, if not insubstantial, role. History was defined by the truth and worth of the subject-matter. Without prescriptive details for historical form, history could therefore be « written » by any illiterate eye-witness of an important event, if he had the inclination — and the scribe — to record it. The *Gesta Francorum et aliorum Hierosolimita-*

norum[1] was the product of just such circumstances. Its subject — the First Crusade — was unquestionably suitable to be « committed to letters ». And if authenticity of historical material was guaranteed merely by an author's visual experience of it (« Quae enim videntur, sine mendacio proferuntur »), there was no doubt of the truth of the *Gesta Francorum* on those grounds either. Only the unsophisticated inelegance of its formal presentation might be faulted.[2] It was therefore predictable that the author would emphatically stress his claims to historical competence. No-one had ever witnessed such events : « tales occisiones de paganorum gente nullus unquam audivit nec vidit » (39). By personal participation this Anonymous was the supremely authoritative historian of all the Crusading events he had witnessed, regardless of the manner in which he chose to present them. Moreover, if unsurpassed now, he would hardly be

[1]   *Gesta Francorum et aliorum Hierosolimitanorum*, ed. L. Bréhier (Paris, 1964).

[2]   It is generally presumed that « unam historiam » which Robert the Monk was ordered to rewrite was our *Gesta Francorum*. The work had been displeasing to his abbot Bernard, he said, because it lacked material on the Council of Clermont, and because it was uncouth in style : « hanc scribere compulsus sum per obedientiam ; quidam etenim abbas nomine Bernardus, litterarum scientia et morum probitate praeditus, ostendit mihi *unam historiam* secundum hanc materiam, sed ei admodum displicebat, partim quia initium suum, quod in Clari Montis concilio constitutum fuit, non habebat, partim quia series tam pulchrae materiei inculta jacebat, et litteralium compositio dictionum inculta vacillabat » (*Roberti Monachi Historia Iherosolimitana, Recueil des historiens des Croisades : Historiens occidentaux* III, p. 721). — Baudri of Dol was equally scathing about « a little book », put together anonymously in rustic fashion, which he rewrote : « Non tamen huic beatae interesse promerui militiae, neque visa narravi ; sed nescio quis compilator, nomine suppresso, *libellum* super hac re nimis rusticanum ediderat ; veritatem tamen texuerat, sed propter inurbanitatem codicis, nobilis materia viluerat ; et simpliciores etiam inculta et incompta lectio confestim a se avocabat » (*Baldrici Dolensis Episcopi Historia Jerosolimitana, Recueil des historiens des Croisades : Historiens occidentaux* IV, p. 10).

surpassed in the future. « Nullus, ut puto, tot prudentissimos milites nec antea vidit nec ultra videre poterit» (8).

The Anonymous was not mistaken about the value of his eye-witness information.[3] In that respect the *Gesta Francorum* has remained authoritative. Its accuracy was, however, directly correlated with the extent of the author's personal involvement in the events. His introductory details were brief and vague, with only such historical preliminaries as an average Crusader might have learned from hearsay. At the divinely appointed time « a strong movement arose throughout all regions of France » to take the Cross. « Cum jam appropinquasset ille terminus quem dominus Ihesus cotidie suis demonstrat fidelibus ... facta est igitur motio valida per universas Galliarum regiones, ut, si aliquis Dominum studiose puroque corde et mente sequi desideraret ... non pigritaretur Sancti Sepulchri viam celerius arripere» (1).

Citations from the New Testament were given more place than the author's unspecific reference to the Clermont Council (« *Apostolicus namque Romane sedis Urbanus secundus ultra montanas partes quantocius profectus est* cum suis archiepiscopis, episcopis, abbatibus, et presbiteris cepitque subtiliter sermocinare et predicare »). The First Crusade was presented in the *Gesta* primarily as the product of groundswell enthusiasm in response to ecclesiastical homilies and directives from the Gospels. « Cumque jam hic sermo paulatim per universas regiones ac Galliarum patrias cepisset crebrescere, Franci audientes talia, protinus in dextra suere scapula cruces inceperunt. » Information concerning the first Crusaders in Constantinople was again vague, and two statements might even be interpreted as contradictory *viz.* that Peter the Hermit was the first to arrive (« Petrus ... primus venit Constantinopolim ») and that he

---

[3]   For a summary of the facts presented by the *Gesta Francorum* see Appendix Two.

found the « Longobards » already there with many others (« illic invenit Longobardos et alios plures congregatos »).

The author's detailed listing of divisions and his résumé of the first few month's events gave place to detailed narrative in the fourth section, however. The « nos » and « nostri » he described were the members of Bohemond's contingent from the Norman duchy of Apulia. Their progress was recorded from a memorable moment of recruitment when Bohemond had crosses cut out from his own cloak, to the Battle of Ascalon. As long as the author fought in Bohemond's army, he gathered information which corrected the particular bias of other eye-witness historians (Tudebod, Raymond of Agiles, and Fulcher of Chartres). But Bohemond's activities in Antioch after the author had proceeded to Jerusalem with Raymond of Toulouse were merely summarized. The narration of the army's march across Lesser Armenia was therefore the author's most valuable contribution by the uniqueness of its detail.

Although personal experience more than any regional preference dictated the author's concentration upon one group of Crusaders, bias was not absent from certain contexts. The author's inability to view Alexius in any other role but that of « infelix imperator » (5) flawed his account of any Crusading negotiations with Constantinople. According to the *Gesta* Alexius was overjoyed (« gavisus ... valde ») when the Turks brutally massacred and dispersed the Christian army at Civitot (2). Further, Alexius was reported to have procured an oath of fealty from Hugh Magnus by duress : « audiens vero dux illius loci hos prudentissimos viros illic esse applicatos, mox mala cogitatio cor ejus tetigit illosque apprehendit ac jussit Constantinopolim imperatori caute duci quo ei fidelitatem facerent » (3). And the same « iniquitous emperor » ordered his Turcopoli and Pincinati to attack and kill the Crusaders : « Et jam cum putarent exire fiducialiter quo vellent, iniquus imperator Alexius imperavit Turcopolis et Pincinatis invadere illos et occidere » (*ibid.*). The crucial detail of Alexius' futile overtures to Godfrey before that order[4] was, however, omitted, probably because it was not known.

Alexius' motives were suspect to the author in all circumstances, and he imputed the worst to the « nequissimus imperator » (6) with a consistency that matched the anti-Greek sentiment of Villehardouin's *La Conquête de Constantinople*.[5] « Tunc imperator, *anxiens et bulliens ira*, cogitabat quemamodum *callide fraudulenterque* comprehenderet hos Christi milites » (6) ; « tunc imperator, *plenus vana*

---

[4]   *Cf*. Albert of Aix : « Post quatuor vero dies legatio Imperatoris processit ad Ducem, quatenus castra moveret ejus causa et precibus, et intra palatia quae in littore Bracchi maris sita erant cum exercitu suo hospitaretur, propter medios algores nivis et hiemis, qui pluviali tempore incumbebant, ne tentoria eorum madefacta et attrita interirent. Cessit tandem Dux et ceteri comprimores voluntati, et amotis tentoriis, per palatia et turritas domos, quae spacium triginta miliariorum, in littore maris comprehendunt, hospitati sunt cum omni exercitu Christianorum. Ab ea die et deinceps, omnem plenitudinem cibariorum et rerum necessarium, ex imperatoris jussu, repererunt et emerunt. — Post paululum dehinc rursus Imperatoris legatio Duci affuit, quae eum ammonuit ad eum ingredi, et ejus verba intelligere. Quod Dux omnino renuit, praemonitus ab advenis civibus de versutia illius ; sed viros egregios illi direxit nuncios : Cononem comitem de Monte Acuto, Baldewinum de Burch, Godefridum de Ascha, ut excusarent eum, et in hoc modo loquerentur : « Godefridus Dux Imperatori magnifico fidem et obsequium. Libenter et optato ad te ingrederer, honores et divitias domus tuae considerarem ; sed terruerunt me plurima mala quae auribus meis de te innotuerunt ; nescio tamen si vel invidia aut odio tui adinventa et vulgata sint ». — Rex siquidem haec audiens, plurimum se de omnibus excusavit, dicens numquam oportere Ducem, vel aliquem de societate, quicquam fallaciae de eo timere aut credere ; sed eum suosque quasi filium et amicos servare et honorare. — Regressi autem nuncii Ducis, omnia quae bene promissa et fideliter ex ore Imperatoris audierant in bonum retulerunt. Verum Dux adhuc minime mellifluis illius promissis credens, prorsus colloquium ejus refutavit. Et sic inter haec nuncia hinc et hinc quindecim dies evoluti sunt», *Liber christianae expeditionis pro ereptione. emundatione, restitutione sanctae Hierosolymitanae ecclesaie*, Recueil des historiens des croisades: Historiens occidentaux, IV (Paris, 1879), pp. 306-7.

[5]   *Cf*., for example, « Cil qui tel murtre faisoit n'avoit droit en terre tenir, et tuit cil qui estoient consentant estoient parçonier del murtre, et, oltre tot ce, [que] il s'estoient sotrait a l'obedience de Rome » (*La Conquête de Constantinople*, para. 224).

et iniqua cogitatione, jussit illos impunitos abire sine ullo timore ac sibi eos Constantinopolim cum magna fiducia adduci ; quos studiose servabat *ut illos ad Francorum nocumenta et obstacula paratos haberet* » (8). Bohemond, on the contrary, was consistently « fortissimus vir » (6) or « doctissimus » (11).

The material was further modified, at least ostensibly, by abridgement. Lists of combatants or casualties were terminated with conventional ignorance-formulae. « In dextera vero parte fuit dux Godefridus et acerrimus miles Flandrensis comes et Hugo Magnus *et alii plures quorum nomina ignoro* » (9) ; « sed fuerunt illic mortui duo de nostris milites honorabiles, scilicet Godefridus de Monte et Willelmus Marchisi filius, frater Tancredi, *aliique milites et pedites quorum nomina ignoro* » (*ibid.*) ; « istas et multas anxietates ac angustias, *quas nominare nequeo*, passi sumus pro Christi nomine et Sancti Sepulcri via deliberanda » (26).

Gaps and inadequacies of information were assumed to be inevitable to the process of eye-witness reporting, and the medieval historian identified them specifically and without apology. The formulae used in the *Gesta* emphasized the impossibility of recording events in their totality. They implied no more apology than had Guillaume de Poitiers's claim to « tenuis prosa ».

They occurred, regrettably, in contexts where accuracy of detail would now be illuminating — what was the exact number of Saracens killed in a given battle, for example, or the correct total of the Arab enemy ? By eye-witness criteria the historian's ignorance of these facts was legitimate. Only divine omniscience could have given fuller control of the material,[6] and divine competence was hardly competition.

---

[6] The difficulty of making numerical assessments *in situ* was a truism which was formulaically stated in many contemporary histories, whatever their stylistic pretensions. Cf. « Unde plateas totius urbis Iherusalem corporibus exstinctis virorum ac mulierum lacerisque membris infantium adeo stratae et opertae fuisse referuntur, ut non solum in vicis, soliis et palatiis,

« Erat autem numerus Turcorum, Persarum, Publicano-
rum, Sarracenorum, Angulanorum aliorumque paganorum
CCCLX milia, extra Arabes, *quorum numerum nemo scit
nisi solus Deus* » (9). Consequently nothing and no-one
could detract from the author's supreme authority over
what he had witnessed.

Significantly, the author did not justify his *brevitas* (if
he considered it as such) on literary grounds. His restraint
was the product neither of complicity with a rhetorically-
trained public (*cf.* Guillaume de Poitiers) nor of inade-
quacy. The *clerc-lai* distinction was, furthermore, irrelevant
since, trained or untrained, the Anonymous knew he was
the best source for the facts. « Omnia que egimus antequam
urbs esset capta nequeo enarrare, quia nemo est in his partibus, *sive clericus sive laicus*, qui omnino possit scribere vel
narrare sicut res gesta est : tamen aliquantulum dicam »
(19). Inadequacies in the total sum of information were to
be blamed upon the impossibility of the assignment, and not
upon the incompetence of the team. And despite all inadequacies the author knew his « aliquantulum » would be
valuable.

The assumption that eye-witness history was valuable
despite its incompleteness implied that the absence of certain details had no particular significance. Facts (« vera »)
contributed to the truth (« veritas ») without being essential
to it. Consequently, the different lexical registers of faith,
truth, and fact could intermingle in surprising combina-
tions, as in the report of the following vision :

> Venit sanctus Andreas rursus, dicens ei : ... « *Scias revera*
> quia quicunque hanc lanceam portaverit in bello nunquam
> ab hoste superabitur. » Petrus vero continuo *revelavit*

sed etiam in locis desertae solitudinis copia occisorum reperiretur innume-
rabilis», Albert of Aix, *Historia Hierosolymitana VI, 30, p. 484* in *Recueil
des historiens des Croisades* IV. Cf. also «Et quum Antiochia, ut dictum
est, capta fuisset, die sequenti multitudo innumera Turcorum circa eam-
dem urbem obsidionem apposuerunt », Fulcher of Chartres, *Historia Ihe-
rosolymitana I, 19, p. 345* in *Recueil des historiens des croisades* III.

mysterium apostoli hominibus nostris. Populus autem *non credebat*, sed prohibebat dicens : « *Quomodo possumus hoc credere ?* » Omnino enim erant paventes et protinus mori *putabant*. Accessit itaque ille et *juravit hoc totum veracissimum*[7] *esse* quoniam ei sanctus Andreas bis in visione apparuerat eique dixerat : « Surge, vade et dic populo Dei ne timeat, sed *firmiter toto corde credat in unum verum Deum* eruntque ubique victuri et infra v dies mandabit eis Dominus talem rem unde leti et gavisi manebunt et, si certare voluerint, mox ut exierint unanimiter ad bellum, omnes inimici eorum vincentur et nemo stabit contra illos » (25).

Since it was eye-witness authority that gave the *Gesta Francorum* its superior claim to truth, no stylistic pretensions were necessarily to be expected. Style was of lesser importance in comparison with the author's unique control of subject-matter. But Isidore of Seville's composite instructions about truth led to stylistic paradox in the *Gesta Francorum* no less than in the *Gesta Guillelmi*. Guillaume de Poitiers, a highly-trained classicist, chose ostentatiously to reject classical models for the bare facts of a « tenuis prosa ». Conversely, the anonymous authors of the *Gesta Francorum*, whose prose was truly « tenuis », occasionally ignored that asset and turned to a more mannered presentation.

The circumstances can be surmised even though they are unverifiable. It would appear that the *chevalier's* clerical collaborator was tempted into embellishment whenever a particular context closely matched a known rhetorical model. Amplification occurred then in speeches or lamentations (10 and 39), in an argument and a letter (21), in a divine invocation (27), and in a description of Antioch.[8] All

---

[7] It should be noted that the superlative form of the adjective results in an attenuation rather than an intensification of the meaning here. Cf. also p. *32*.

[8] Bréhier considers this description to be a late interpolation : « Enfin deux chapitres nous paraissent constituer des interpolations ajou-

but two of these amplifications were short, but their formal techniques differed markedly from the rest of the text. They demonstrate a literary background that an unlettered soldier could never have acquired. And, in addition to their rhetorical devices, they contain unexpected and extraneous references to the Amazons (« ultra Amazonia flumina », 21), the Furies (« insanis aut furiis es plena », 22), and even an exclamation in Greek by the Turkish emir (« micro Francos echome », 20).[9] Significantly, it was amplifications like these which contained most of the *Gesta*'s assertions of truth.

In the *Gesta Francorum* an assertion of truth served to reinforce material that was extraneous to the factual narrative of verifiable events. It asserted credibility with, or without, a justificatory reason : « Haec verba credenda sunt quia plures ex nostris viderunt » (29). In the preceding quotation the material was guaranteed as credible because several of « our men » saw it. Thus numberless white hosts on white horses with white standards rode down the mountain to rescue the Crusading army, led by Saints George, Mercurius, and Demetrius.

The eye-witnessing of visions was several times guaran-

tées plus tard à l'ouvrage. L'un (chap. xxvii) raconte l'entrevue du comte Etienne de Blois après sa fuite d'Antioche et reproduit de longs discours qui ne sont pas dans la manière de l'Anonyme ; ce morceau paraît remonter à l'époque de la querelle entre Bohémond et Alexis (1103-1111) et pourrait bien être une pièce de propagande destinée à soulever les Occidentaux contre l'empire byzantin. L'autre (chap. xxxii) est une description d'Antioche intercalée bizarrement entre le récit de l'expédition de Raimond de Toulouse contre Albara et celui du siège de Marra. Ces deux morceaux rompent la suite des événements et, bien qu'ils figurent dans tous les manuscrits, on doit les considérer comme ajoutés à la rédaction primitive » (p. vii).

[9] The authenticity of this Greek quotation has also been questioned, but in Bréhier's view, « il n'y a aucune raison pour mettre en doute, comme le veut Hagenmeyer, (édition des *Gesta*, p. 303, n. 43), la véracité de la réflexion de Firouz. Le grec était resté en Orient une langue internationale et beaucoup de Turcs le parlaient » (p. 107, n. 1).

teed as truth, especially when the seer's integrity could be established. The verb « scire » was then conjoined to prophecy as if prophecy were acquired fact (see above, p. 29). Similarly, the significant juxtaposition of « verum » and « credere » occurred in the context of a vision of Christ, his mother, and St. Peter when they promised support for the Crusaders. The priest who was the « eye-witness » of that vision guaranteed its content by offering trial-by-ordeal. His survival from a suicidal jump would demonstrate that he had truly seen the vision, that he had truthfully reported its contents, and that its contents were true — such was the ambiguity of « hoc esse verum » in the following passage : « Seniores, *si hoc non creditis esse verum,* sinite modo me in hanc scandere turrim mittamque me deorsum ; si vero fuero incolumis, *creditis hoc esse verum*, sin autem ullam lesionem fuero passus, decollate me aut in ignem projicite me » (24).

Truth was invoked three times for the vision of the Holy Lance. St. Andreas guaranteed : « scias revera quia quicunque hanc lanceam portaverit in bello nunquam ab hoste superabitur » (25). Then the visionary guaranteed the truth of his vision : « accessit itaque ille et juravit hoc totum veracissimum esse quoniam ei sanctus Andreas bis in visione apparuerat » (*ibid.*), citing St. Andreas' admonition to believe in « unum verum Deum ».

The mendacious Stephen of Chartres introduced his false report to Alexius with a guarantee of truth: «scias revera quoniam capta est Antiochia » (27). Bohemond's brother, « miles honestissimus », was however able to distinguish truth from falsehood by an examination of the witness's credibility — « imprudens Stephanus » was challenging the word of « Deus verus ».

The Turks were represented as making the same sort of truth assertion about a falsehood. Their statement about their « true » lineage was followed by an authorial assertion of « veritas » :

> Verum tamen dicunt se esse de Francorum generatione et
> quia nullus homo naturaliter debet esse miles nisi Franci et
> illi. Veritatem dicam quam nemo audebit prohibere : certe,
> si in fide Christi et Christianitate sancta semper firmi fuis-
> sent et unum Dominum in trinitate confiteri voluissent Dei-
> que filium natum de virgine, passum et resurrexisse a mor-
> tuis et in celum ascendisse suis cernentibus discipulis conso-
> lationemque Sancti Spiritus perfecte misisse et eum in celo
> et in terra regnantem recta mente et fide credidissent, ipsis
> potentiores vel fortiores vel bellorum ingeniosissimos nullus
> invenire potuisset (9).

In another amplified digression Kerboga's mother
pleaded with her son to abandon his attack upon the Christians. An assertion of truth provided her introduction and
also the substance of her oration :

> « Fili, suntne vera que audio ? ... Audivi quia bellum vis
> committere cum Francorum gente. » Ait ille : « Verum
> omnino scias... »
> « Hoc autem, carissime, in rei veritate scias, quoniam isti
> Christiani filii Christi vocati sunt et, prophetarum ore, filii
> adoptionis et promissionis et secundum Apostolum heredes
> Christi sunt, quibus Christus hereditates repromissas jam
> donavit dicendo per prophetas: A solis ortu usque ad occa-
> sum erunt termini vestri et nemo stabit contra vos. Et quis
> potest his dictis contradicere vel obstare ? » (22).

The consistent distinction, Scriptural in origin,[10] that the
Gesta Francorum made between the « vera » and the « veritas» of its material was not unusual. It persisted throughout
medieval historical tradition to confound subsequent ages
for whom facts were observable, truth subjective. In the
Gesta Francorum truth assertions demonstrated that facts
were often the province of divine omniscience alone and
were beyond human reach (« nemo scit nisi solus Deus »),

---

[10] Cf. « Perdam sapientiam sapientium, et prudentiam prudentium
reprobabo. Ubi sapiens ? ubi scriba ? ubi conquisitor huius saeculi ?
Nonne stultam fecit Deus sapientiam huius mundi ? » (*Ad Corinthios* I, I,
19-20).

whereas the truth was accessible and could not be controverted. By the appending of a Christian credo to a description of the Turks, truth was revealed. By the same means
the author's undue admiration of a heathen army was
neutralized, and alien subjects made to serve a useful purpose. It was, after all, the « veritas » more than the « vera »
of the First Crusade which justified the usefulness of the
Anonymous' history.

Chapter Three

Truth and Propaganda

Villehardouin, marshal of Champagne, had contributed
to the organization of the abortive Fourth Crusade, and to
him the subject was impressive by its magnitude, «une des
plus doutoses choses à faire qui onques fust ». There was,
furthermore, a lesson for posterity in its history *viz.* the
necessity of obedience to leadership. « Onques nus
n'eschiva l'ost de Venise que mals ou ontes ne l'en venist. Et
por ce si fait que sages qui se tient devers le mielz. »

From a disinterested eye-witness such sentiments would
be less suspect than from a leader. Villehardouin's inconsis-
tent handling of his material and his scattered assurances of
« verité » provide useful evidence for the view that Villehardouin's purpose was justificatory. Despite the fact that *La
Conquête de Constantinople*[1] was composed in the vernacular by an illiterate at a time when all preceptive theories
about history were in Latin, and when medieval history was
dominated by rhetoric, the work fulfilled admirably the original function of rhetoric : oral persuasion.

« Sachiez » was the first word of *La Conquête de Constantinople*. The didactic imperative occurred without
explanation, dedication, or preamble. It was used sixty
times thereafter to reinforce certain facts, and each occurrence effectively constituted a truth claim. It implied an

---

[1]   Geoffrey de Villehardouin, *La Conquête de Constantinople*, ed. E.
Faral (Paris, 1938).

author who knew the truth authoritatively and an audience who could be persuaded to accept more than sixty propositions on that authority. Each occurrence selected for emphasis certain facts out of the totality. It is therefore by a comparison of the totality of facts presented[2] with the « sachiez » - introduced facts that truth and propaganda are best separated in *La Conquête de Constantinople*.

In the three initial paragraphs of introductory fact « sachiez » introduced Fulk of Neuilly as the inspiration of the Fourth Crusade (1), stressed his fame (2), and the youthfulness of two royal Crusaders : Thibaut of Champagne and Count Louis of Blois (3). Thereafter its use was spasmodic. « Sachiez » was absent in some portions of the narrative, then peaked in others. The audience was urged by Villehardouin's « sachiez » to accept the following assertions as true :[3]

There was much emotion when the Franco-Venetian agreement was signed (the gravity of the leaders' sworn agreement) (31) ;

Odo, Duke of Burgundy, would not join this expedition, and could have done better than to refuse the leaders' request (castigation of those who did not cooperate with the leaders' plans) (39) ;

There was much emotion when the Crusaders left their home and friends for the Crusade (praise for the heroes) (47) ;

More than three hundred catapults, mangonels, and siege weapons were loaded on the ships bound for Zara (assurance from the author, the Crusade's provisioner and negotiator, that the Venetian fleet was well-equipped and was worth its exorbitant cost) (76) ;

[2] The facts presented by *La Conquête de Constantinople* are summarized in Appendix Three.

[3] English translations are mine. Phrases in parenthesis have been provided to link the material with central themes in *La Conquête de Constantinople*. Occasionally « de voir » was appended to the didactic imperative.

The Franco-Venetian mêlée was the most tragic event that ever occurred in an army (damage from discord) (89) ;

There was no peace in the army (damage from discord) (100) ;

If God had not loved this expedition, it would not have been able to hold together, so many sought to damage it (damage from discord, God's favor for the leaders) (104) ;

Many of the Crusaders viewed Constantinople for the first time, not believing that such a wealthy city could exist in all the world (the importance of Constantinople as a Crusading target) (128) ;

There were many fine knights in the fifth battalion (praise of Villehardouin's battalion) (151) ;

The siege of Constantinople was one of the most hazardous enterprises ever undertaken (importance of Constantinople as a Crusading target) (157) ;

Anyone who wished to enter Constantinople had to negotiate the chain that was attached to the Galata tower (importance of sea tactics and, therefore, importance of the Venetians) (159) ;

In the Galata capture James of Avesnes was hard-pressed and gravely wounded (praise of heroes) (160) ;

The army had no rest (magnitude of the enterprise, praise of heroes) (165) ;

They had not enough provisions for three weeks of siege-warfare (praise of heroes, the necessity for heavy plunder) (165) ;

The galleys did not dare to land (praise of the doge who heroically urged them on) (172) ;

God never rescued any army from such extreme peril as on that day (God's favor for the leaders' plans) (181) ;

Even the toughest soldier was joyful at the conquest of Constantinople (recognition of the importance of Constantinople, appreciation of God's favor) (181) ;

Many of the soldiers went to view the city (importance of Constantinople) (192) ;

All of the Greeks accepted the emperor as he toured the

region, except John of Wallachia (appropriateness of the Crusaders' candidate, castigation of an enemy) (202) ;

John had captured almost half of the territory on this side of the straits of St. George (threat of the enemy) (202) ;

The messengers' mission was extremely perilous because Greeks are treacherous (praise of heroes, castigation of the enemy) (211) ;

The clergy's promise of papal pardon was a great comfort to the leaders and to the Crusaders generally (assurance that the Church approved the leaders' policy and that the papal excommunication would not therefore be irrevocable) (225) ;

Not one of the eighty soldiers in the deserting company escaped death or capture (castigation of those who did not cooperate with the leaders) (231) ;

The Crusading army had more casualties than the Greeks that day « for their sins » (Divine punishment formula, the results of non-cooperation) (238) ;

There were some who would have liked the current to carry the ships away from the city (castigation of the non-cooperative) (239) ;

The death of Count Louis of Blois was a great loss to the army (praise of heroes — Louis was both cousin and nephew of the reigning king, and had connections with Villehardouin's Champagne) (245) ;

All the Constantinople booty was not handed over (castigation of the non-cooperative) (254) ;

When the leaders had divided the booty, they paid out of their own share fifty thousand silver marks to the Venetians, and shared one hundred thousand of it out among their own men (proper behavior of the leaders in distributing the booty) (254) ;

Anyone convicted of theft was duly punished — many men were hanged (proper behavior of the leaders in distributing the booty) (255) ;

The Electors of the Emperor of Romania were the object of

much attention (importance of the new imperial appointment) (260) ;

Many rich robes were made for the coronation (importance of the new imperial appointment) (261) ;

Geoffrey the Marshal was shown much gratitude after he resolved the dispute between Boniface and Baldwin (praise of a hero, importance of concord) (287) ;

The men in the army were much distressed at the death of Master John of Noyon, chancellor of Baldwin of Flanders (praise of a hero) (290) ;

Things went well for the Franks in their conquest of Poemaninon, Lopadium and Polychna, and by God's help they accomplished their will in the area (God's favor for the leaders' planning) (320) ;

James of Avesnes's army was nearly destroyed at Corinth, but repulsed the enemy with the help of God (praise of heroes, God's favor for the leaders' planning) (332) ;

There was no pity for those of Renier of Trit's household who, having abandoned him in a dangerous situation, were themselves deservedly captured and beheaded by John of Wallachia (castigation of the non-cooperative) (345) ;

The leaders were very fearful when they heard that one company had irresponsibly separated itself from the expedition to take a quicker route, and they thought that all the remainder they had left at Adrianople would be lost (castigation of those who did not cooperate with the leaders) (368) ;

The Crusaders in Constantinople were very fearful at the news of the Rusium defeat, thinking certainly that they had lost the whole territory (magnitude of the Romania enterprise, the heavy odds) (411) ;

All the strongholds captured by John were totally destroyed and their inhabitants exiled to Wallachia (castigation of the enemy's barbarism) (420) ;

Within a five-day radius of Constantinople nothing remained to be ravaged except the French-occupied strongholds of Bizye and Salymbria (castigation of the enemy's barbarism, demonstration of the civilizing, stabilizing nature of the French protective occupation) (421) ;

The Crusaders were now in an inferior position, having retained only two cities outside Constantinople (magnitude of the Romania enterprise, the heavy odds, praise of heroes) (421) ;

Everyone considered John's retreat from Demotika a great miracle (God's favor for the leaders' planning) (432) ;

Those who went to rescue Renier of Trit (Villehardouin was among them) were on a dangerous mission (praise of heroes) (436) ;

Renier of Trit and his household were overjoyed to see their rescuers (appreciation of heroes) (438) ;

The recapture of John's captives was no small enterprise (praise of heroes) (448) ;

The emperor Henry and the barons (Villehardouin was one) had a heavy responsibility (overwhelming magnitude of the Romania enterprise, praise of heroes) (460) ;

It was considered a great miracle that the powerful John of Wallachia would withdraw from a city that was nearly his — Adrianople (God's favor for the leaders' planning) (475).

....

The recurring directives above created a climate of persuasion in Villehardouin's third-person past-tense *narratio rei gestae*. His audience was continually urged by this imperative to accept certain aspects of the Fourth Crusade as undeniably true. To the modern reader each occurrence of « sachiez » should serve as an indicator of extra-factual elements that Villehardouin has added to past events.

«Sachiez » urged the potential value of the controversial Constantinople diversion, the worth of the Venetians as Crusading allies, the barbarism of the Greeks, the heroism and civilization of the Franks, the magnitude of the leaders' « Romania » enterprise, the Divine favor that accompanied the Crusaders, the destructive and irresponsible effect of those who were unwilling to cooperate with the leaders. and the blame that attached to all who plotted against a divine and heroic expedition.

Individual Crusaders were sometimes singled out by the « sachiez » directive. Thibaut, count of Champagne, was twice given prominence, presumably because of Villehardouin's Champagne loyalties, and because Thibaut was a cousin and nephew of the contemporary king. Louis, count of Blois and Chartres, was similarly well-connected and similarly highlighted. The listing of names from the Champagne battalion (of which Villehardouin was a member) ended with a « sachiez » assurance of the quality of that contingent. Special tribute was paid by this means also to one of the expedition's leaders, James of Avesnes, for his heroism when he was mortally wounded in the face by an enemy lance.

Conversely, timidity (e.g. of the galleys before the doge's heroic exhortation), brutality (e.g. of John of Wallachia), and perfidy (e.g. of the Greeks) were deplored through « sachiez » assertions. The morality of military obligations was consequently stressed. It was a morality that reinforced the case which Villehardouin was constructing by a skilful presentation of his facts. His narrative methods were as logical as his negotiating strategies. The build-up of events was punctuated at critical moments by a didactic directive, synchronizing author's and audience's reactions. With an inevitability that was almost geometric, crime resulted in punishment, virtue in reward, bad faith in failure. Each « sachiez » instruction added an argument to Villehardouin's special pleading.

The « sachiez » interventions could occur at once-remove in passages of direct speech. Given that direct speech was generally realistic fabrication or reconstruction, the target of the author's persuasion remained unchanged. It was Villehardouin's public and *not* the participants of the Fourth Crusade who were actually addressed. The twelve direct-speech assertions presented as truth in this subtle manner reinforced general themes of *La Conquête de Constantinople*.

Messengers from Alexius urged that Alexius' offer to bring Romania under the jurisdiction of Rome was the finest agreement ever offered to anyone : « Et sachiez que si halte convenance ne fu onques mes offerte a gent » (94). The religious value of the leaders' tactics was thereby underlined by Villehardouin although (or perhaps, because !) their support of Alexius' dynastic claims had caused widespread defection.

The leaders' political viewpoint was soon presented again in a dramatized debate between the two factions (in which only the leaders were granted oratorical privileges, while the abbé of Vaux-de-Cernay was reported in indirect speech). « Et sachiés que par la terre de Babiloine ou par Grece iert recovree la terre d'oltremer, s'ele jamais est recovree » (96).

The doge of Venice was made the mouthpiece for another of the leaders' decisions when, in the author's succinct French prose, he urged that the army reprovision off the nearby islands instead of foraging overland : « Sachiez, se nos alons a la terre ferme, la terre est granz et large » (130).

« Sachiez » urged upon Constantinople's inhabitants (and Villehardouin's audience) the Crusaders' right to invade the Greek city : « Sachiez nos ne venimes por vos mal faire, ainz venimes por vos garder et por vos deffendre se vos faites ce que vos devés » (146). They well knew (« Bien savez ») the faithlessness of their present emperor.

By « sachiez » Alexius twice urged the necessity for one of the (various) unpopular decisions of the leaders *viz.* to support Alexius' rule for a further year : « Sachiez que assez gens me mostrent bel semblant qui ne m'aiment mie » (194) and « Sachiez, se vos me laissiez, li Grieu me heent por vos » (195).

The same means introduced a vindication of the leaders' eventual decision to abandon Alexius after the year of delay : « Et saches tu que il te reprovent le servise que il t'ont fait » (213) and « se vos nel faites, sachiez que, des hore en avant, il ne vos tienent ne por seignor ne por ami » (214). « Sachiez » introduced Boniface's petulant threats to Emperor Baldwin : « Et sachiez vos de voir, je n'irai mie avec vos » (277). It introduced the leaders' threats to both of them : « Et sachiez que il vos mandent que il ne souffriroient la guerre en nulle fin » (293). « Sachiez » urged appeals from two besieged cities (to which help was forthcoming on the leaders' recommendation) : « Sachiez que, se tu ne seccors la cité del Dimot, que ele ne se puet tenir plus de .viii. jorz » (428) and « Sachiez que cil de Chivetoth sunt assis per mer et per terre ; et se vos nes secorrez hastivement, il sunt pris et mors » (465).

When « sachiez » urged a point of view, the point of view was invariably that of the leaders. When used in direct speech, it dramatized the importance of certain issues. It introduced the unverifiable, or it elicited appropriate emotions from Villehardouin's public. They were assured that a *tremor of awe* afflicted the whole army at the sight of Constantinople, that the Venetian agreement was signed *with pious respect*, that the Pope ratified it *willingly*, and that the Galata tower was captured *with pride*. None of these attitudes was attested or attestable. Even divine omniscience could not have given authority to Villehardouin's assurances that God was on the leaders' side, when historical events had so clearly demonstrated a contrary « truth ». The process of imputing sentiments to key personages or groups was, however, useful to obtain acceptance for the capture of Constantinople by a Franco-Venetian alliance. It encouraged hostility towards the Greeks who were, after all, despicable by nature. *De quabus rebus disputatum et disputandum.*

As for the issue that caused open controversy within the army — the leaders' distribution of Constantinople's wealth — its sensitivity can be assessed by a comparison of Robert de Clari's accusations with Villehardouin's demonstrations.

The persuasive function of « sachiez » in the latter is tested to the fullest degree by its unusual frequency :

ROBERT DE CLARI :

Ensi faitement si commenchierent l'avoir a embler, si que on ne departi onques au quemun de l'ost, ne as povres chevaliers, ne as serjans qui l'avoir avoient aidié a waaignier, fors le gros argent, si comme des paieles d'argent que les dames de la chité portoient as bains. Et li autres avoirs qui remest a partir fu cachiés si males voies com je vos ai dit, mais totes eures en eurent li Venicien leur moitié, et les pierres precieuses et li grans tresors qui remest a partir ala si males voies comme nous vous dirons aprés.[4]

VILLEHARDOUIN :

Assemblez fu li avoirs et li gaains, et *sachiez* que il ne fu mie toz aportez avant: [quar assez en i ot de ceus qui en retinrent, seur l'escomeniement de l'apostole. Ce qui aus mostiers fu aportez] assemblez fu et departiz des Franz et des Venisiens par moitié, si cum la compaignie ere juree. Et *sachiez* que, quant il orent parti, que il paierent de la lor partie .L. mil mars d'argent as Venitiens ; et bien en departirent .CM. entr'als ensemble par lor gent. Et *sachiez* comment : .II. serjanz a pié contre un a cheval, et .II. serjanz a cheval contre un chevalier. Et *sachiez* que onques on ne out plus por altesce ne por proesce que il eüst, se ensi non com il fu devisez et fais, se emblez ne fu.

Et de l'embler cel qui en fu revoiz, *sachiez* que il fu fait grant justise ; et assez en i ot de penduz. Li cuens de Sain Pol en pendi un suen chevalier, l'escu al col, qui en avoit retenu. Et mult i ot de cels qui en retindrent, des petiz et des granz ; mes ne fu mie seü. Bien poez savoir que granz fu li avoirs : que, sanz celui qui fu emblez, et sanz la partie des Venitiens, en vint bien avant .CCCC. .M. mars d'argent, et bien .X.M. chevaucheüres, que unes que autres. Ainsi fu departiz li gaienz de Costantinople com vos avez oï (254-5).

When Villehardouin's learned-on-command truths are separated from his facts, *La Conquête de Constantinople* takes on the appearance of an elaborate rhetorical con-

⁴ Robert de Clari, *La Conquête de Constantinople*, ed. P. Lauer (Paris, 1924), p. 81

struct. The process of manipulation need not always have been intentional, but may have been encouraged by the narrative tradition Villehardouin inherited and the circumstances in which he wrote. An author's need to dictate all material to a scribe may in itself incite to persuasion, and the act of composition be a trial performance in front of a captive listener. Whatever the reasons for Villehardouin's stylistic practices, there is no doubt that they fulfilled brilliantly the aim of every rhetorician : audience persuasion.

Villehardouin's conviction of the greatness of his Crusade was thus urged upon his audience. He also made several explicit truth guarantees whose persuasive potential should have been immense because of Villehardouin's personal participation in events. However, he exploited his advantage only three times, and in paradoxical contexts. The ambiguous function of the truth guarantee is nowhere more apparent than in *La Conquête de Constantinople*.

In paragraph 120 Villehardouin validated his authority as a historian by advertising (truthfully) the uniqueness of his own Crusading experience — he had been present at all the councils. He reinforced these qualifications of personal experience with a character reference which may have been somewhat less than truthful : he had never intentionally lied. « Et bien testimoigne Joffrois li mareschaus de Champaigne, qui ceste oevre dita, que ainc n'i menti de mot a son escient, si com cil qui a toz les conseils fu. » He then, however, rendered this specific and potentially persuasive introduction useless by a detail that was not only irrelevant to councils but also to the facts of his history : « que onc si bele chose ne fu veüe ; et bien sembloit terre qui deüst conquerre. » The assertion, if accepted literally, implied omniscience and omnipresence. It depended upon aesthetic comparisons made by a hypothetical deity. But the statement was obviously neither literal nor « true ». And the second component of this conventional hyperbole (« this certainly looked like a conquering fleet ») was even less worthy of its guarantee.

The next truth claim was deployed similarly in a context to which Villehardouin's experience was irrelevant : « Et ce tesmoigne Joffrois de Villehardoin li mareschaus de Champaigne, qui ceste ouvre traita, que plus de .XL. li distrent par verité que il virent le confanon sain Marc de Venise en une des tors et unc ne sorent qui l'i porta » (174). Here Villehardouin's eye-witness experience guaranteed the hearsay evidence from an unidentified group who swore they had seen a demonstration of God's favor to the Venetians.

Villehardouin's third and final statement about truth would again have required omniscience to make it authoritative : « Et bien tesmoigne Joffrois de Vilehardoin li mareschaus de Champaigne, a son escient par verté, que, puis que li siecles fu estorez, ne fu tant gaainié en une ville » (250). Villehardouin, planner and negotiator in the Constantinople diversion, was not in fact suggesting any systematic comparison of history's plundered cities. He aimed rather at creating a monument for posterity out of Constantinople's capture. His work therefore propagandized for his heroes against the rest. His last emphatic truth claim was a dogmatic and pragmatic validation of the leaders' planning for the conquest of Constantinople.

QUOD ERAT DEMONSTRANDUM

Chapter Four

Truth and the Pagans

Pagan histories were not harmful when they dealt with useful things. Pagan poetry had been characterized — and damned — by Isidore of Seville for its embellishment of truth : « officium autem poetae in eo est ut ea, quae vere gesta sunt, in alias species obliquis figurationibus cum decore aliquo conversa transducant » (*Etymologiae* VIII, vii, 10). Pagan history was, on the other hand, acceptable for Christian readers because of its basic content of truth. « Historiae gentium non inpediunt legentibus in his quae utilia dixerunt. »

Medieval translators of classical history accepted Isidore's tenets, and justified their craft and their products accordingly. One of the most influential, the anonymous compiler of *Li Fet des Romains*,[1] quoted the *Etymologiae* on multiple occasions, referring to it with reverent familiarity as « l'Escriture ».[2] His compilation of Caesar's *Bellum Gallicum*, molded the pagan material in various ways to meet Isidore's criteria of utility and truth.[3]

[1] *Li Fet des Romains* ed. L.-F. Flutre and K. Sneyders de Vogel (Paris, 1938).

[2] As, for example, in the definition of « basilisk » : « Le roi des serpenz l'apele *l'Escriture* » (p. 608, 1. 12) for Isidore's « rex serpentium » (*Etymologiae* XII, iv, 6).

[3] Since the material to be presented by the translator is not his eyewitness experience (as in Chapters One to Three), but an inherited and varied corpus, it is not productive to compare the facts of *Li Fet des Romains* with the translator's presentation of the facts. This chapter will

The translator specified his aims in the prologue : « Por ce escrivrons nos ci ilueques les gestes as Romains qui, par lor sens et par lor force et par lor proesce, conquistrent meinte terre; car en lor fez puet en trover assez connoissance de bien fere et de mal eschiver.» And if the message to do good and to avoid evil seems somewhat too vague to be utilitarian, it did not remain so. Throughout *Li Fet des Romains* Christian sense was imposed upon pagan confusion, as the translator sifted « good » from « bad » in the name of truth.

Each of his truth statements introduced a reworking of the classical historians so that they could be sold as useful products for thirteenth-century consumption. And because one of the most harmful ingredients in classical history was its pre-Christian paganism, *Li Fet des Romains* must of necessity neutralize this by a process of positive reinforcement of truth, and negative comment concerning error. The translator's dogmatism about truth concerned the « veritas » and not the « vera » of his source-material.

An opposition was assumed to exist between pagan attempts to prove truth (« li ancien disoient ... li ancien voloient prover ») and contemporary knowledge/belief (« nos creons »), which was based upon the true evidence (« tesmoing ») of Holy Scripture. The ancients had tried to prove, for example, that Mount Parnassus was the center of the earth, because Jupiter's two eagles had met there after one had flown east and the other west : « Li encien disoient que cil monz estoit en mi le monde et li nombliz de la terre. Par ce le voloient prover que Jupiter lessa .ij. aigles aler, l'une d'orient et l'autre d'occident, et vint l'une contre l'autre en volant, tant que eles s'entrecontrerent ilueques en ce mont » (p. 452, lines 2-6).

The first didactic reminder of the erroneousness of the pagan view was given in the phrase « *voloient* prover »,

therefore analyze the translator's modifications of his sources when they are accompanied by assertions of truth.

which implied a lack of success in the misguided attempt at scientific demonstration. The translator then inserted a comment on the irrelevance of pagan surmise in a Christian dispensation, and made an unequivocal statement about truth in which knowledge converged upon belief : « whatever the ancients may have thought, we believe, on the evidence of Holy Scripture, that Jerusalem is in the center of the world, for it was in the center of the world that Jesus Christ preached and died » (« que que li encien en cuidassent, nos creons par le tesmoign de Sainte Escriture que Jherusalem est en mi le monde, car en mi le monde preescha Jhesucrist et morut », p. 452, lines 6-9).

Julius Caesar's factual description of Druid religion could conceivably have been harmful to a medieval audience also. It explained a pagan system with objective interest, and it showed paganism to be potentially useful to its society. Belief in the transmigration of souls, for example, eliminated the fear of death, and was a great incentive to military valor : « in primis hoc volunt persuadere non interire animas, sed ab aliis post mortem transire ad alios, atque hoc maxime ad virtutem excitari putant metu mortis neglecto » (*Bellum Gallicum* VI, xiv, 5).[4]

The translator simplified his source-material by obscuring the connection between metaphysical belief and its social consequences. His simple statement « enmes ne muerent pas, mes quant l'une oissoit d'un cors, si entroit en autre », (p. 222, lines 28-9) was followed by (but not linked to) a bland statement that was appropriate to either Christian or Druid contexts : « vertueus apeloient celui qui nule poor avoit de mort » (line 30).

Julius Caesar's explanatory account of Druid practices was labelled as Julius Caesar's opinion : « c'en est li quidiers Julius Celsus » (line 28). Any metaphysical beliefs that the Druids might have affirmed as true were relegated to the

---

[4]   Julius Caesar, *Bellum Gallicum* (Leipzig, 1968).

category of misguided notions that obtained before Christianity : « moutes choses ensaignoient des estoiles, dou firmament, de la nature des choses que l'en puet veoir as ielz, de la force et de la poesté des diex qui estoient creü a cel tens ainz que Nostre Sire nasquist » (p. 222, line 31 - p. 223, line 2).

Explicit dissociation from the pagans could be carried further. The translator actively encouraged his public to reject what he had translated from the *Bellum civile* IX, 7-9,[5] where Lucan had put Pompey's spirit in the fire-cleansed regions of the ether among heroes. The translator made a derisory intervention on that subject : « believe that who will ! » He then excused his inclusion of the erroneous material on the grounds that he was merely translating what was there : « Mes li espirist, ce dist Lucans, — qui le veust si l'en croie, — s'en ala vers la lune en air ; por itant con Lucans le dist le vos rendons » (p. 574, lines 4-6).

On some occasions the translator's ignorance of Stoicism led him to misinterpret Lucan's metaphysics as Christian truth, however. He saw Lucan's reference to the world's final conflagration not as Stoicism's purificatory fire-worship, but as a surprising premonition concerning the Last Judgment. « 'Cesar ne sousfri que cist fussent ars, au meins ne lor pot il pas tolir le conmun feu qui sera en la fin dou monde, que tuit ardront avec le ciel et la terre.' Ci samble il par ces paroles que Lucans seüst et creïst aucune chose de la fin dou monde » (p. 543, lines 1-5).

He anticipated any questioner who might wonder how Lucan could have acquired this knowledge — the source was probably the writings of the Sybil. « Se l'en demande conment il le sot, l'en puet dire que il l'avoit leü es escriz Sebile qui en parla. De ce feu meisme ce dist David : 'Feus ardera devant Damedieu quant il vendra au jugement, et forz tempeste sera entor et environ' » (*ibid.*, lines 5-9). The

---

[5]   Lucan, *Bellum civile* (Cambridge, 1969).

categorization of Lucan's metaphysics as Christian because of their (Stoic) paganism may be ironic. The accident contributed, nevertheless, to the overall purpose of extracting truth from pagan history.

In his continuing attention to the process of sifting error from truth, the translator obviously used as one of his criteria Isidore's distinction between history and fable : « item inter historiam et argumentum et fabulam interesse. nam historiae sunt res verae quae factae sunt ; argumenta sunt quae etsi facta non sunt, fieri tamen possunt ; fabulae vero sunt quae nec factae sunt nec fieri possunt, quia contra naturam sunt » (*Etymologiae* I, xliv, 5). The category of « fabulae » had been well represented in the ninth book of Lucan's *Bellum civile* where, for example, the Perseus myth attributed the serpents of Libya to scattered blood-drops from the Medusa's severed head (*Bellum civile* IX, 619-733).

Such spontaneous generation of vipers was obviously incompatible with the Creation according to Genesis. The translator used the incident to remind his audience that the best evidence for truth was divine testimony. He then gave an Isidorean explanation for rejecting Lucan's material. Its reasoning was fourfold — and less effective in the sum of its parts than any one argument might have been in isolation. He chose not to clutter his book further with this material, he said, (« nos n'en volons cest livre encombrer de plus ») first, because it had not the appearance of truth (« por ce que ne samble pas veritez ») ; second, because Lucan himself did not believe it (« Lucans meîsmes nel croit pas ») ; third, because the translator wished to follow the order of true history (or the real story !) (« volons suivre l'ordre de la vraie estoire »), knowing by the evidence of Holy Scripture that God created serpents (« nos savons bien par tesmoign de Seinte Escriture que Damlediex cria serpenz des le conmencement dou monde ») ; and, fourth, because it was in accordance with Nature (« naturels chose est ») for serpents to thrive in a warm rather than in a cold climate.[6] Nature was therefore in alliance with Holy Scripture as a criterion for truth, and Lucan's fable was demonstrated as mendacious because it did not conform with either. « Fabulae vero sunt quae nec factae sunt nec fieri possunt, quia contra naturam sunt ».

In the above passage the translator claimed also that he was employing the technique of « brevitas » to produce truth. He expunged much of Lucan « por ce que ne samble pas veritez ». Other explicit claims of truth through « brevitas » occurred in contexts of error or unedifying material. For example, the translator claimed that a complete catalogue of pagan oracular pronouncements would not be given because of its length. « All that the devils uttered to the Saracens through images and sacrifices before Christ's coming » (p. 452, line 29) would not therefore be listed in *Li Fet des Romains*.

The magic of pagan sorceresses elicited a similar comment : « longue chose seroit a dire tote la merveille qu'eles savoient fere » (p. 496, line 33). Exhaustive treatment of augury was also declined : « d'autres signes que longue chose est a dire » (p. 510, line 29).

Since all important material from the source had already been translated before the ostensible abridgement of these subjects, the translator's interventions must be analyzed for other messages e.g. « this pagan subject does not deserve too much attention ». An accepted stylistic formula was once more being exploited for purposes other than its ostensible one. The « brevitas »-formula in *Li Fet des Romains* drew attention to truth, and distracted from pagan error.

The truth-fable opposition in *Li Fet des Romains* was not restricted to questions of religion. « According to the fables » centaurs were half-man and half-horse, but « according to the truth » they were the first men who ever

---

[6] *Li Fet des Romains*, p. 604, lines 10-17.

learned to ride on horseback. « Selonc les fables, ce sont demi home et demi cheval ; mes selonc la verité, cil de la terre monterent primes sor cheval, et cil qui ainçois les virent cuiderent que ce fust uns meïsmes cors de l'ome et de cheval, si les apelerent en lor langage Centors ; ce ne fu autre chose » (p. 397, lines 2-6).

The interpolation demonstrates a search (by both the source — a gloss[7] — and by our author) for a truth that will be naturalistic rather than « contra naturam ». It demonstrates also the medieval identification of « fable » with « lie ».[8] What the gloss had labelled « mentita », the translator rendered as « fables », and opposed to « verité ».

Between « historiae » and « fabulae » Isidore had described the intermediate genre of « argumenta », « quae etsi facta non sunt, sed fieri tamen possunt». It was probably on the authority of that definition that the translator included in *Li Fet des Romains* fictional episodes that now seem inappropriate within a serious historical compilation. An examination of the translator's statements about truth clarifies his intentions for these interpolations, and demonstrates that to him they were *probabilia*, not truth.

The inventions occurred when the sources were inadequate in their information. Lucan's account of the Civil War terminated frustratingly before the translator could achieve his goal of writing Caesar's biography from birth to

---

[7] «Illic enim nati dicuntur Centauri; *mentita* autem ideo dixit quia volunt illos primos equis esse usos ad sedendum, et de longinquo visos creditos esse Centauros », Bc, Lb, W[1] C G[1]. Quoted by L.-F. Flutre and K. Sneyders de Vogel in their commentary (*Li Fet des Romain* II, p. 161).

[8] The medieval interpretation of « fabula » as antithetical to truth and as synonymous with « mensonge » appears to have dominated all other possibilities of classical usage, as far as the translator was concerned. For that reason he made nonsense of Lucan's « victoribus ipsis / Dedecus et numquam superum caritura pudore / *Fabula* » (*Bellum civile* VIII , 604-6) (« a *tale* disgraceful to the Victor himself, and one destined to shame the heavens forever ») when he rendered it as « Et ce samble *fable*, et Cesar meïsmes i pot avoir grant honte » (p. 564, lines 5-6).

death. At the end of Lucan's tenth book the translator complained several times of the brevity, obscurity, and confusion of his sources : « Lucans s'em passe ci elecques si briement, que nus ne puet savoir certain ordre de l'estoire par chose que il en die. Suetoines meïsme⟨s⟩ n'en redist qui a conter face» (p. 645, lines 1-3) ; « ceste chose que nos avons ici contee ... touche Lucans si tres briefment et si obscurement, que nus ne puet estre certefiez de la verité ne de l'ordre de l'estoire par chose que il en die » (p. 651, lines 25-9) ; « voirement Herodotus et Berosus et Oppius et Hircius cist quatre em parolent en lor estoires, mes mout confusement, et sont a chief de foiz contrere » (p. 652, lines 10-11).

Since no-one could be guaranteed of truth by reading extant versions of the Battle of Alexandria, the translator acknowledged that he had resorted to invented probabilities. By his criteria this procedure was closer to the truth than was the absence of all detail. It was not possible, he said, that seasoned soldiers would have allowed themselves to be defeated without much conflict and much struggle (p. 522, line 14).

Thus by a curious twist of logic, truth in *Li Fet des Romains* could sometimes[9] be identified with expansion, and invention preferred to misleading brevity. The nature of the interpolated passages would not be misunderstood by contemporaries because of the translator's explicit comments. Concerning his version of Caesar's treatment of Ptolemy after Alexandria he made a significant claim to *probable* truth by negativing his truth guarantee : « *nos ne l'afermons pas por voir* ; mes espoir il le feïst bien, se li tres granz resoinz venist, et li trenchast avec la teste quant il fust fors de tote esperance d'eschaper » (p. 642, lines 22-4). By using hypothetical past subjunctives for all actions and by refusing to affirm the truth (a positive statement not being reversed, necessarily, by the addition of a negative !) the

[9]   Cf., however, p. 52.

translator enjoyed a double advantage. He combined the refusal to be held responsible for the truth of certain material with the suggestion that the material *probably* was true. He notified his audience that Lucan was not the author of these details, that he himself *was*, and that, despite that acknowledgment, his version had to be closer to the truth than any other version available.

His explicit acknowledgements of invention were reinforced by stylistic features which, since they were reserved for the interpolated episodes, served to categorize further the translator's different modes of truth. Knowing that to his contemporaries poetry implied fiction,[10] he interspersed considerable fragments of epic verse throughout his invented battles. The adoption of an epic style, appropriate to fantasy, labelled the invention as invention, but the attenuated truth guarantee introduced ambiguity by legitimizing the invention as probable truth. The use of the truth guarantee had acquired a new sophistication in this game with the audience.

That audience was necessarily obliged to play a different role in the passages of invention. It was directly invited to participate in, and to visualize, the battle scenes: « lors veïssiez abatre bois et aporter a drecier les terreauz » (p. 406, line 5). Lacking Roman eye-witnesses, the translator forced his audience into vicarious participation. They became the sympathetic guarantors of events in Caesar's Rome, as the translator ensured for his narrative both verisimilitude and drama. Nevertheless, throughout such passages, the subjunctive mood (« veïssiez », « oïssiez », « il le feïst bien »)[11] clearly distinguished historical *probabilia* from historical fact.

---

[10] See the frequent coupling on « fable » and « chançon » in such formulaic phrases as « De si grant dol n'oï onques nus parler n'en fable n'en chançon » (p. 584, lines 8-9) or « l'en n'en trove rien n'en fable n'en chançon » (p. 632, line 21).

[11] See the quotation on p. 54.

The medieval public was not alone in this role of imaginary eye-witness to the truth. The translator once ventured to guarantee his classical source-material by inventing a hypothetical Roman as its guarantor. Misled by the third-person narrative of the *Bellum Gallicum* and by an inscription on the manuscript concerning Julius Celsus Constantinus,[12] he replaced Julius Caesar with an all-seeing companion. He legitimized the authority of this puzzingly omnipresent eye-witness to Caesar's every move by a gratuitous and seemingly innocuous addition : « mes nos en demandames assez as païsanz de Bretaigne, *dist Juliens qui ce livre fet, car nos i fusmes avec Cesar* » (p. 184, lines 24-25). The interpolation was the translator's most disastrous exploitation of the truth guarantee, although no medieval audience was in a position to recognize the inauthenticity. The dual appearance of Julian *alias* Caesar as himself and as his own guarantor exemplified the mendacious potential of the truth guarantee in medieval narrative.

Other remodellings of the source were less audacious, although equally revealing. The original Julius Caesar had investigated reports that areas of Britain near the Isle of Man had thirty-night-long midwinters without sunlight. On-the-spot inquiries had brought him less information than water-measurements from a water-clock. By the latter means Cesar had discovered that nights were indeed shorter in those areas of Britain than they were on the Continent : « nos nihil de eo percontationibus reperiebamus, nisi certis ex aqua mensuris breviores esse quam in continenti noctes videbamus » (*Bellum Gallicum* V, xiii, 4). Caesar's original inquiries about the truth of his information had thus proceeded from the anonymous written statements of « nonnulli scripserunt » through oral questioning (« percontationibus ») to scientific measurement (« aqua »).

---

[12] « Julius Celsus Constantinus uc legi » was inscribed on the group of manuscripts which provided the translator with his source.

The relative importance of these various stages was radically altered in the medieval text. The subject under inquiry (now, incidentally, a thirty-day period without night !) was, according to the translator, found by Caesar in the writings of historians : « Entre Bretaigne et Illande a plusors isles dont *aucun ystorien distrent en lor escriz* que en aucun tens de l'an n'i anuite de .xxx. jors continuex » (p. 184, lines 22-24). Thus it had the authority of « Scripture ». Testimony was then sought on the spot, and sources were identified by the medieval translator as the local inhabitants of Britain : « nos en demandames assez *as païsanz de Bretaigne* » (*ibid.*, line 24). The inquirors were given a new and spurious authority by being named (albeit as someone else !).

The omission of all reference to the water-measurements shifted the weight of evidence to the experiences of the non-existent but named eye-witnesses. « Mes voirement nos perceüsmes » symbolized the paradoxes presented by medieval truth-statements. Given credibility by (anonymous) written authorities and by the testimony of a spurious eye-witness, « voirement nos perceüsmes » ignored the limited scientific truth that Caesar had been able to acquire by objective measurement. « Truly we perceived », although untrue, was nevertheless the best possible guarantee for Caesar in the thirteenth century.

Eye-witness testimony could be presented as conclusive even when it was at third-remove. Suetonius had vouched for the Capuan tomb prophecy of Caesar's death by citing as his authority Cornelius Balbus, Caesar's personal friend : « cuius rei, ne quis fabulosam aut commenticiam putet, auctor est Cornelius Balbus, familiarissimus Caesaris » (*Vitae* I, lxxxi, 2).[13] The French translator was even further from the evidence, yet he too vouched for the truth — this time of what Suetonius had said that Cornelius Balbus had said that the prophecy had said : « Ne tienge nus

---

[13] Suetonius, *Vitae* I (Stuttgart, 1967).

ceste parole a fable, car Suetoines dist que Cornilles li Bau-
bes, qui mout fu privez de lui, Cesar, le tesmoigne ensi » (p.
739, lines 5-7).

In this mass of second-hand and sometimes third-hand
material, there were certain factual contexts where the
translator ventured to intervene with his own assertions
about the facts (« vera »). His interventions, introduced by
« voirement », « voirs est », « veritablement », or « vraiement », merit analysis to determine what — if any — contribution has been made in them to the historical accuracy of
Caesar's biography.

The first was an explanatory expansion of Isidore's description of an amphitheater : « Il avoit une grand place a
Rome ceinte de haut mur, que l'en apeloit cercle ou amphi-
teaitre ; car *voirement* theaitres n'est pas reonz, ainz est
come demi roe, mes li amphiteaitres est reonz come cer-
cles » (p. 17, line 23 - p. 18, line 1). The source of the translator's detailed knowledge about amphitheaters was not
divulged, but was presumably a gloss. Glosses were the
translator's unnamed and disparate authorities which, together with Isidore of Seville, he categorized unspecifically
as « l'escriture ».

Apart from demonstrating that the amphitheater's so-
called circle was not round, the authority of the gloss's written word could « prove » truly that Pompey was without
covetousness («l'en puet bien prover par escriture que il fu
sanz covoitise, car l'en troeve lisant que, quant il ot prise
Jerusalem, il entra ou temple ... onques n'em leva un seul
besant », p. 571, lines 19-21), or that Centaurs were men
(see above p. 52).

Unfortunately, written authority was not an infallible
guarantee of truth — glosses sometimes provided conflict-
ing information. The translator then attempted to resolve
the disagreement by logic, as in his ingenious explanation
for the place of Caesar's assassination : « La corz Ponpee
ou il fu ocis fu estoupee. Se l'en troeve en aucun leu que il fu
ocis ou Capitoile, ce n'est pas descorde, car ou c'onques li

senaz s'assembloit ce estoit bien Capitoiles » (p. 744, lines 10-13).

If such resolution was not possible, he opted arbitrarily for one set of facts over another. His version might for all that be introduced as truth : « *voirs est* que li archier et li arbalestier Pompee en ocioient mout la sus en mi l'aitre del temple, si que il se merveilloit coment il pooient endurer, et de ce que, por nul meschief, ne lessoient lor sacrefices a fere ne lor osfrendes » (p. 69, lines 23-26). This detail of the Jews slaughtered by Pompey's bowmen at the altar of their synagogue came from the *Bellum Judaicum*, which the translator used here in preference to Petrus Comestor. The phrase « voirs est », which introduced the above unpalatable truth about the translator's hero Pompey, was accompanied by no indication of a changed source and by no explanation, therefore, for the change.

In the siege of Gergovia Vercingetorix's position on the right slope of the fortified mountain was guaranteed true : « *voi(e)rs est* que Vercingetorix et li soen estoient logié ou destre pendant de la montaigne ou la cité seoit » (p. 265, lines 31-2). The explanation concerning Vercingetorix's position was, however, the translator's inaccurate rendering of Caesar's more complex tactical explanation in the *Bellum Gallicum* (VII, xliv). It added nothing but error.

After the fatal combat invented for the Gallic hero Camulogenus who, in Caesar's combat, was inactive because he was « prope confectus aetate » (*Bellum Gallicum* VII, lvii, 3), the translator asserted it was true that the army lost their assurance at that point. « Si com Camulogenus fu ocis et cil dou senestre cor le virent chaoit, *voirs est* que mout em perdirent de lor seürté » (p. 278, lines 15-16). Again, « voirs est » was employed for a context of non-fact.

« Voirement » introduced a slightly different presentation of the facts of *Bellum Gallicum* (VIII, xxiv, 1) concerning the disintegration of the Gallic opposition to Caesar. To Caesar the Gallic flight from the towns reinforced the fact of his successful domination of Gaul : « bellicosissimis gentibus devictis Caesar cum videret nullam iam esse civitatem quae bellum pararet quo sibi resisteret, *sed nonnullos ex oppidis demigrare*, ex agris diffugere ad praesens imperium evitandum, plures in partes exercitum dimittere constituit.» The translator introduced the same information adversatively with «voirement»: «voirement auquant François l'aloient fuiant d'un chastel a autre et d'un recet a autre poι son conmandement eschiver a present » (p. 312, lines 6-8). The slight twist presented the bleak historical fact of « French » flight in as favorable a light as was possible.[14]

In a clarification concerning the true identity of Brenno, the translator moved from the known « facts » of Arthurian legend to the unknown exoticism of Caesarean Rome. « Veritablement cil Brenno qui fu au tens Artu ne fu pas li premerains dont la citez de Sens fu renomee, mes uns autres qui assist Rome et la prist jusq'au Capitoile au tens Camillus qui fut conciles de Rome ançois que Marius et Silla fussent, qui furent ançois que Cesar ne Pompees eüssent point de pooir » (p. 317, lines 4-9). The interpolation indicates to what extent the *Historia regum Britanniae* and *Brut* had precedence over the *Bellum Gallicum* as accepted and acceptable truth.

By another « vraiement » the translator interposed a judgment of daring authorial omniscience concerning Crassus « who had been truly most covetous ». « Et vraiement Crassus ot esté mout covoitex, si que il gita bien dou tenple de Jherusalem ou il avoit entré, entor .ij. mile talenz d'or qui la estoient en conmande » (p. 338, lines 29-32). The context for the « vraiement » was again fiction or, at least, fabrication — the entire section had been put together by the translator, and fused to the end of Caesar's eighth book.

« The truth » about the campaigning Caesar's continued absence from Rome was encapsulated in the following

---

[14]   For a full acount of the translator's pro-Gallic modifications see Jeanette Beer, *A Medieval Caesar* (Geneva, 1976), Chapter Five.

invented summary which the translator twice guaranteed as true :

> *Voirs est* que, quant il ot demoré .v. ans antiers es besoignes dou conmun, et il ot meinte bataille fete, et conquise grant partie de France, tant come il en a entre les alpes des porz d'Espaigne et les monz de Genoive, et de Genoive jusqu'au Rin et jusqu'au Ronne, il ne vost pas aler a Rome por renoveler et por reçoivre sa baillie dou senat ; ainz li fu vis que il n'avoit rien fet qui a gloire li deüst torner oncore ne a renomee. Por ce vost demorer autres .v. ans oncore, tot sanz le congié dou senat, tant que il eüst conquis le remanant de France. Mes *voirement* il manda as tribuns de Rome qui estoient si ami, que il parlassent au pueple et requeïssent la baillie por lui, car ne li sembloit pas biens se il lessast la besoigne que il avoit commenciee, avant qu'il l'eüst tote achevee. Li pueple(s) le vost mout volentiers, que que fust dou senat (p. 339, lines 11-25).

In that summary the complexities of candidature, the role of the Roman people and the tribunes, and Caesar's own politics have all been misrepresented. The reduction of history to the simple truth of Caesar's inordinate ambition has, however, contributed to the comprehensibility and didactic value of Caesar's life. Antiquity's « vera » have provided illustration for the « veritas » of the human condition. THE TRUTH has been served by falsehood.

The translator manipulated the « vera » similarly on p. 351, line 7 (where « voirement » introduced material from a gloss), on p. 466, line 22 (where « voirement » confirmed a truism), on p. 544, line 10 (where « voirement » confirmed that the gods hated Thessaly), and on p. 700, line 31 and p. 706, line 3 (where battle details were supplied from the translator's imagination).

The translator's explicit truth interventions should therefore be regarded with suspicion wherever they occur. To extract utility from paganism they modified the source-material whenever it controverted Christian dogma. They imposed a Christian meaning upon the arbitrariness of

Roman history. They used Caesar's political machinations as demonstrations of lust and ambition. They supplemented inadequate sources with inspiring *probabilia* to propagandize for a French Augustus' new France. They occurred in contexts of subjectivity, hypothesis, error, and sometimes mendacity. Had it not been for these attempts to ascend from the «vera» to the «veritas», *Li Fet des Romains* would surely have qualified as the most scholarly presentation of classical antiquity in the thirteenth century.

Chapter Five

The Truth of Love, the Truth of Fable, and the Truth

Truth guarantees occurred occasionally in early fictional narrative. Marie de France claimed to have selected for narration those Breton *lais* which she knew to be true : « Les contes ke jo sai verrais, / Dunt li Bretun unt fait les lais, / Vos conterai assez briefment » (*Guigemar,*[1] lines 19-20). The promise is cryptic by the richness and vagueness of its suggestion. If it was intended for literal acceptance, two plausible interpretations present themselves.

Marie's « ke jo sai verrais » implied, perhaps, that she assessed her material by the criterion of human experience. Within the narrative context of each *lai* such knowledge was invariably a knowledge of the heart rather than the head. « Une chose sai jeo de veir : / Il quidera ke jeo me feigne » (*Laüstic*, lines 130-131). The « truth » that Guigemar told to his lady was the story of his symbolic wound (*Guigemar,* lines 311-332). The maidservant's « truth » was that she had seen and taken pity on a pale stranger on a magic ship (*ibid.*,

---

[1]   Marie de France, *Lais* (Oxford, 1944). It is assumed in this chapter that Marie de France was the author of all three works discussed in this chapter. For a different view see Richard Baum, *Recherches attribuées à Marie de France* (Heidelberg, 1968).

lines 276-286). The « truth » of the mischief-making wife in *Le Fresne* was her twin conception many years before (*Le Fresne*, lines 471-2). Other uses of « verité » to denote the happenings of love occur in *Le Fresne*, lines 47 and 75, *Yonec*, lines 282 and 537, *Milun*, line 439, and *Eliduc*, line 1017.

It is not clear whether the personal element implied by « ke *jo* sai verrais » should be further emphasized. But regardless of whether Marie intended to allude to her own experiences of love, her constant concern was to demonstrate the contemporary appeal and the relevance of her *lais*. To that end she made frequent authorial interventions which, far from being mere *chevilles*, justified and explained seeming departures from the norms of human behavior : « N'est merveille se il s'esmaie, / Kar grant dolur out en sa plaie » (*Guigemar*, 197-8) ; « Ne vus esmerveilliez neent : / Kar ki eime mut lealment, / Mut est dolenz et trespensez » (*Chevrefoil*, lines 21-3). Certain uses of the present tense in introductions and conclusions showed the immediacy of the *lais* by setting them in an « eternal » present : « L'aventure d'un autre lai, / Cum ele *avient*, vus cunterai » (*Lanval*, lines 1-2) ; « Issi *avient* cum dit vus ai. / Li Bretun en firent un lai » (*Equitan*, lines 311-2).

A more literary explanation of « les contes ke jo sai verrais » was suggested by A. Ewert in his note to that line : « *verrais* in the sense that they are authenticated by tradition. This gives all the more force to the following line with its explicit reference to *lais* composed by the Bretons (i.e. Celts) — whatever may have been the provenance of the narrative materials they exploited. The reference to a written source or model is reminiscent of the similar conventionalized invoking of 'gestes' and 'livres' by authors of epics and romances, but is not necessarily to be classed here as a mere conventional trick. »[2] In the case of *Chevrefoil*,[3] where dif-

[2] *Lais*, ed. A. Ewert, p. 165.

[3] For discussion of the different versions of the Tristan legend in

fering versions of the Tristan legend are known to have been current, authenticity may well have been one of Marie's preoccupations. But there are other *lais* where Marie showed a complete disinterest in the precise details that would identify an « authentic » version. Her text contains numerous disclaimers to temporal precision, for example. Guigemar was with his lady a year and a half, « ceo m'est avis » (*Guigemar*, line 535) ; Lanval's encounter with the queen occurred, « ceo m'est avis, meïsmes l'an, / Aprés la feste seint Johan », (*Lanval*, lines 209-220) ; Milun stayed in Britanny one full winter, « ceo m'est avis » (*Milun*, line 381).

Infallibly correct nomenclature was apparently equally irrelevant to the « truth » of the *lai*. Marie's casualness in that regard is indicated by her use of the phrase « ceo m'est avis » (« Laüstic ad nun, ceo m'est vis », *Laüstic*, line 3) and by her use of an inability-to-relate topos : « En Bretaine ot quatre baruns, / Mes jeo ne sai numer lur nuns », (*Chaitivel*, lines 33-4). By these means Marie skimmed lightly across the surface of historical detail toward weightier matters.[4]

It is difficult therefore to assess the technical grounds upon which Marie might have wished to claim authenticity for her *lais*. It seems preferable to interpret Marie's assertions of truth as narrative ploys rather than as literal assertions. Like the king's councillor in *Bisclavret* who urged cre-

Marie's time see Adams, A. and T.D. Hemmings, «*Chèvrefeuille* and the Evolution of the Tristan Legend », *Bibliographical Bulletin of the International Arthurian Society* XXVIII (1976), 204-13 ; Hofer, S. « Der *Tristanroman* und der *Lai du Chievrefueil* der Marie de France, » *Zeitschrift für romanische Philologie* LXIX (1953), 129-31 ; Schoepperle, G. « *Chievrefoil* », *Romania* XXXVII (1909), 196-218 ; Williman, J.P., « The Sources and Composition of Marie's Tristan Episode », *Studies in Honor of Tatiana Fotitch* (Washington, 1972), pp. 115-27.

[4] Villehardouin would borrow the same narrative technique for his summaries of factual details, especially military names, in *La Conquête de Constantinople*.

dence for legend (« Meinte merveille avum veü / Que en Bretaigne est avenu », *Bisclavret*, lines 259-60), Marie coaxed her audience into a temporary suspension of disbelief by her narrative techniques. The geographical details[5] and the historical assurances that she scattered through the *lais* gave a patina of actuality to fiction.

They guaranteed four *lais* specifically. *Bisclavret* concluded with an assurance that the werewolf episode actually happened : « L'aventure ke avez oïe / Veraie fu, n'en dutez mie », (*Bisclavret*, lines 315-6). Corroboration of its truth was to be found in the fact that women from the treacherous wife's lineage were born without noses : « Plusurs des femmes del lignage, / C'est verité, senz nes sunt nees », (*ibid.*, lines 312-3). Incontrovertible evidence that the story of *Les Deux Amanz* had actually happened in Normandy was the fact that a wondrously high mountain exists there : « Jadis avint en Normendie / Une aventure mut oïe ... / Verité est ke en Neustrie, / Que nus apelum Normendie, / Ad un haut munt merveilles grant» (*Les Deux amanz*, lines 1-2 and 7-9). Citing unspecified Celtic sources, oral and written, for *Chevrefoil*, Marie twice asserted the truth of that episode[6] : « Asez me plest e bien le voil / Del lai que hum nume Chevrefoil / Que la verité vus en cunt », (lines 1-3) and « Dit vus en ai la verité / Del lai que j'ai ici cunté » (lines 117-8). *Eliduc* also contains a double claim concerning the truth of the narrative that had been extracted from a legendary *lai* : « De un mut ancien lai bretun / Le cunte e

---

[5] For information on Marie's use of place-names see E. Brugger, « Über die Bedeutung von *Bretagne, breton* in mittelalterlichen Texten », *Zeitschrift für französische Sprache und Literatur* XX (1898), 79-162 and « Eigennamen in den *Lais* der Marie de France », *ibid.* LXIX (1927), 201-52, 381-484; L.-F. Flutre, *Table des noms propres avec toutes leurs variantes figurant dans les romans du moyen âge écrits en français ou en provençal et actuellement publiés ou analysés* (Poitiers, 1962) ; E. Hoepffner, « La Géographie et l'histoire dans les *Lais* de Marie de France », *Romania* LVI (1930), 1-32.

[6] It is unfortunate that this episode is extant only in Marie's version.

tute la reisun / Vus dirai, si cum jeo entent / La verité, mun escient », (lines 1-4) and « L'aventure dunt li lais fu, / Si cum avient, vus conterai, / La verité vus en dirrai », (lines 26-8).

These truth assertions made a substantial contribution to the success of the *lai* by adding plausibility to its incredible elements : werewolves, magic ships, and love potions. Marie's assurance that she was relating those *lais* which « she knew to be true » was particularly useful in the absence of any authoritative written source. « Li livres » here was initiating rather than inheriting an accepted written corpus. The author therefore chose to validate her book by a formula that had previousy justified eye-witness history. She claimed the truth of Celtic legendary fiction by her personal experience of it.

If the truth guarantees in the *Lais* were cryptic by their vagueness, the cited authorities for the *Fables*[7] were baffling despite Marie's precision : « Esope apele um cest livre, / kil translata e fist escrivre, / de Griu en Latin le turna. / Li reis Alvrez, ki mult l'ama, / le translata puis en Engleis, / e jeo l'ai rimé en Franceis », (Epilogue, lines 13-18). It is fortunate, in view of Marie's misconceptions concerning « Romulus »[8] and « Esope », that she made no claim which suggested even remotely the question of authenticity. She aligned herself with the fabulists of antiquity whose concern was with a different sort of truth : « Par moralité escriveient / les bons proverbes qu'il oieient / que cil amender s'en poïssent / ki lur entente en bien meïssent », (Prologue, lines 7-10). Whether or not « *bons* proverbes » implied any selectivity in the transmission process, there is no doubt that it was now moral truth that interested Marie : « Que cil amender s'en poïssent ki lur entente en bien meïssent ».

[7]   Marie de France, *Fables*, ed. Karl Warnke (Halle, 1885).

[8]   According to the Prologue of the *Fables* « Romulus, qui fu emperere, / a sun fiz escrist e manda / e par essample li mustra / cum se deüst contreguaitier / que hum nel peüst engignier » (lines 12-5).

The didacticism which promoted that truth was necessarily as complex as the fabulist tradition itself. Truth must be distinguished from falsehood (*De leone aegrotante*, p. 226).[9] But truth could vary according to individual perception of it (*De mure et rana*, p. 11). Truth could be platitudinous and repetitive or it could be vital (*De lupo et nauta*, p. 261). It could be exploited (*De lupo regnante*, p. 96), and cynically misrepresented (*De muliere et proco eius*, p. 145). Truth could be personal (*De lupo et agno*, p. 8). In society « veir dire » was usually dangerous (*De lupo regnante*, p. 96 ; *De simiarum imperatore*, p. 115).

No less paradoxical was Marie's inherited view of the fabulist's responsibility to truth. On the one hand, fable was an *essample*, an encapsulation of moral truth (see previous p. 67 above). On the other hand, fable was by definition non-truth, « quae nec factae sunt nec fieri possunt ».[10] Truth was to be found in the « essample », « reprueche », « respit », and « fable » (*De cornice et ove*, p. 135), but « fable », « mençunge », and « sunge » were synonyms of one another — the truth was found elsewhere :

> Par essample nus vuelt aprendre
> que nuls ne deit niënt entendre
> a fable, ki est de mençunge,
> n'a peinture, ki semble sunge ;
> c'est a creire dunt hum veit l'uevre,
> ki la verité en descuevre
> 　　　　　　(*De leone et homine*, p. 129).

---

[9]　The Latin titles are provided for easier identification of the fables.

[10]　For another expression of Isidore's view that truth was not incumbent upon the fabulist, see the dedication of the Avianus fragment (Bib. Nat. ms. lat. nouv. acq. 1132) : « Dubitanti mihi, Theodosi, quonam litterarum titulo nostri nominis memoriam mandaremus, fabularum textus occurrit, quod in his urbane concepta falsitas condeceat, et non incumbat necessitas ueritatis ... Loqui uero arbores, feras cum hominibus geîmere, uerbis certare uolucres, animalia ridere facimus, ut pro singulorum necessitatibus uel ab ipsis animis sententia proferatur. »

Marie's translation *L'Espurgatoire Seint Patriz*[11] was dedicated exclusively to Christian truth. The repetitive « veir », « pur veir », and « veirement » served as constant reminders of that truth which was necessarily unverifiable on earth. Only Adam had known everything about the Terrestrial Paradise : « Par seint espirit entenduns / D'altre vie, mes ne poüns / Saveir le tut certeinement ; / Adams le sout veraiement », (*L'Espurgatoire*, lines 1717-20). But Sir Owein, by his descent to Purgatory and his visit to the Terrestrial Paradise, and Saint Patrick by his revelation of the purgatorial pit, became similarly enlightened. The sources of this highest truth were revelations, visions, and man's inner awareness of God, therefore. « Plusurs almes veirement, / Einz que des cors puissent partir / Veient que lur est a venir : / Plusurs par revelaciun, / d'altres par avisiun, / U par lur dreite conscience, / Sulunc iço qu'il unt licence. / Plusurs des almes veirement / Veient, devant lur finement, / Avisiuns e sunt ravies ... / Il veient espiritelment / Ço que semble corporelment » (*L'Espurgatoire*, lines 62-8). A subsequent narration of those experiences would presumably impart whatever truth had been revealed.

The immediate source for Marie's translation was Henry of Saltrey's *Tractatus de Purgatorio Sancti Patricii*. She called it variously « le livre de l'Espurgatoire » (line 2298), « ceste escripture » (lines 30 and 47), « nostre escrit » (141), « li escriz » (421), « en escrit » (504), and « li livre » (4, 806, 1404). Of the above references not even « li livre » conformed with the tradition of an unquestioned and unquestionable authority. Indeed by a reversal of the conventions Marie occasionally vindicated « li livre » rather than being vindicated by it. By her explanation Gilbert of Louth had received his facts about the torments of Purgatory from Owein and the monk of Basingwerk, who had personally

---

[11] Marie de France, *L'Espurgatoire Seint Patriz*, ed. T. Jenkins (Philadelphia, 1894 ; rep. Geneva, 1974).

experienced them. Gilbert had reported them to Henry of Saltrey who, like Marie, affirmed their truth in a series of truth guarantees :

> Gileberz cunta icel fait
> A l'autor quil nus a retrait,
> Si cum Oweins li out cunté,
> E li moignes dunt ai parlé :
> Ço que jo vus ai ici dit
> E tut mustré par mun escrit.
> E puis parlai a dous abbez :
> D'Irlande erent bons ordenez.
> Si lur demandai de cel estre,
> Si ço poeit veritez estre.
> Li uns affirma que veirs fu
> De l'espurgatoire et seü
> Que plusur humë i entrerent
> Qui unques puis ne returnerent.
> En cel an meïsmes trovai
> Un evesque a qui jo parlai.
> Nevuz fu al tierz Seint Patriz
> Qui cumpainz ert Seint Malachiz.
> Florenciëns aveit a nun ;
> Il me cunta en veir sermun
> Que l'espurgatoire ert assis
> En s'eveschié e la fu quis.
> Ententivement li enquis
> Si ço fust veirs, que l'en ert vis :
> E il me dist : « Certeinement,
> Que c'esteit veirs » ... (lines 2057-82)

Marie's repeated assurances were directed primarily towards the material of the revelation. An explicit guarantee of Henry's rendering was less insistent. It noted merely that the subject of life after death was of general concern : « Plusur cuveitent a saveir / Des almes, *ci nus dit pur veir*, / Cument eles issent des cors / E u vunt quant eles sunt hors » (lines 93-6). The implied selectivity of that «ci nus dit pur veir », whether intentional or not, did little to confirm the text's overall validity.

In fact « li livres » was of less importance to Marie than was its presumed ultimate source : revelation. Insofar as certain individuals could be guaranteed to have witnessed « veritas », their narrations of the revelation — and all translations of the narrations — were thereby guaranteed. The only possible demonstration of the truth of *L'Espurgatoire* would of course be its efficacy towards salvation in an after-life.

VERITAS LIBERABIT VOS.

Chapter Six

The Game of Truth

Guillaume de Machaut used an assertion of truth as the title of *Le Livre du Voir-dit*.[1] Thus his entire poetic narrative was guaranteed as true[2] — and literary historians have been arguing over its « truth » ever since. In fact, all the contradictions inherent in the medieval truth conventions have been realized and brought to brilliant culmination in this literary game.

Guillaume had already juxtaposed personal experience and traditional formulae in previous works. His lyrics, for example, juggled truth and the *lieux communs*. The customary opaqueness of the poet's « je » had always protected personal identity while ostensibly revealing it. Contemporaries appreciated Guillaume's skill in maintaining that equilibrium. King René's epitaph on Guillaume — « si eus le renom / D'estre fort embrasé de penser amoureux »[3] — made no attempt to distinguish between the factual truth of Guillaume's life and Guillaume's poetic stance. *Guillaume was renowned for being* empassioned with love's meditation. The ambiguity of the epitaph was proper

[1] Guillaume de Machaut, *Le Livre du Voir-dit*, ed. Paulin Paris (Paris, 1875).

[2] The title might mean also « a true composition », « a true testimony » « a verdict », « what was truly said », « a deposition under *voir-dire* injunction ».

[3] *Oeuvres du roi René*, ed. M. le comte de Quatrebarbes (Paris, 1846), p. 128.

homage to an ambiguous art in which truth was interwoven with fiction. This was convention in the raw, reality *à la mode*.

The transference of ambiguously personal techniques to extended narrative was more demanding. Even the earliest of Guillaume's works contained, however, jesting juxtapositions of truth and convention, as in *Le Dit dou Lyon's* : « *En ce dous temps dont je vous cont, / Dou mois d'avril le jour secont, / L'an mil trois cens quarante deus* ».[4] The passage is now useful to date Guillaume's work, but for Guillaume's contemporaries it was a game of whimsy. A timelessly conventional lyric introduction to Spring love had been unexpectedly joined to a historically precise moment : « April's second day in the year one thousand three hundred and forty-two ».

Guillaume combined reality and convention again in similar fashion one hundred lines later : « Si vi en l'onmbre d'un arbril, / Droitement le tiers jour d'avril, / Un batel ... » (lines 139-41). A sentence of dream-reality was fixed in time by the shock-line « precisely on the third day of April ».

Guillaume's jarrings of the audience's expectations were not clumsy *chevilles*. His confrontations of truth and the formulae in *Le Dit dou Lyon* were its very subject, as an aged lover played *chevalier* with self-deprecating humor. (The citation of chivalric heroes and, in particular, the *Neuf Preux* in lines 1315 ff. preceded a mischievous suggestion that contemporary *preux* visit those particular countries that Guillaume himself had toured with Jean de Luxembourg).

A didactic disquisition on the nature of love became a realistic enumeration of frivolous and demanding lovers. The sheer weight of their anti-courtly example was suggestive, and was not counteracted by the short concluding

---

[4]   *Le Dit dou Lyon*, ed. E. Hoepffner (Paris, 1906), lines 31-3.

statement : « Mais toutes pas teles n'estoient » (line 1691).
A mere seven lines encompassed all the paragons of virtue :
« Car maintes dames le faisoient / Einsi comme Amours le
devise, / Sans mal engien et sans feintise, / De fin cuer loial,
sans meffaire, / Dous, humble, courtois, debonnaire, / Par
franche liberalité / Et de fine pure amité » (lines 1692 ff.)
The game of love had been appreciated ideally and demonstrated to be in conflict with reality.

Truth confronted convention again when peasants were
unexpectedly included in Guillaume's list of different styles
of loving (lines 1537 ff.). A love-conversation between
Robin and Marote impressionistically conveyed by its
unpolished abruptness the rudimentary love-habits of the
unsophisticated : « Par le cuer bien, je t'aime, sote, / Et se
n'i say raison pour quoy » (lines 1546-7). And if such
attempts at truth revealed more about court assumptions
about peasants than about peasants themselves,
Guillaume's purpose was obvious — truth à la mode.

Another literary precedent — the exploitation of religious terminology for courtly contexts — also acquired new
boldness in Le Dit dou Lyon when false lovers were por-
trayed as worse than Judas : « pis que Judas qui se pandi »
(line 1210). Lovers then by implication played the role of
Christ, and the chevalier made a mock prayer beseeching
the destruction of all treacherous lovers. He then invited
participation in a new Easter liturgy : « Grant meschëance
leur avengne ! / Dites : « Amen ! Dieu en souveingne ! »
(lines 1211-1).

Such transferences from sacred to profane might have
appeared blasphemous. Yet if the chevalier in the role of
Christ made antithetical parody of the dying Christ's
« Πάτερ, ἄφες αὐτοῖς » by praying « Father, do not forgive
them », his identity with Christ was thereby negated, the
message was self-contradictory, and Guillaume's use of the
conventions remained ambiguous.

Guillaume's use of falconry in Le Dit de l'alerion was
similarly allusive, as didactic exempla attacked contempo-

rary reality. Like *Le Roman de Renqrt, le Dit de l'alerion* held in balance symbolic and real, animal and human, never quite espousing, never quite abandoning either.

In *Le Livre du Voir-dit*, however, the game of truth dominated all other artistic intentions. The use of the truth guarantee as title tested the formula's potential to the ultimate degree. Such ambiguity as had been associated previously with the truth tradition must now be sustained throughout. Truth must be poised in suspension if the mendacity of the truth devices was to be exploited fully.

Guillaume's true-life story was a love-affair with a platitude : Toute-belle. That lady's true identity was revealed/concealed in anagram. The medium for Guillaume's true-love history/story was both prose (the medium of fact) and poetry (the medium of fancy). The actuality of love was proved by poetry. « Le vrai amant » embodied « veritas » and « fidelitas » and, since the one was demonstration of the other, « true » love's ambiguities were made manifest. Ideal imagination became actual fact. Truth was fiction, and fiction was truth.

Guillaume's true-false propositions were not alien to an audience that was accustomed to the creatively conventional, the rhetorically personal, or the individually universal. Unfortunately, now, the cult of ambiguity is no longer fashionable, and *Le Livre du Voir-dit* is frequently the subject of ponderous analyses which establish once for all Toutebelle's « true » identity. Now Guillaume's assertions of truth must be either true or false. They cannot be both and neither.

Truth was not only Guillaume's title — it was his *leit-motiv*. « Voir », « voire », « voirement », « vrai », « vrayement », « veritable », « veritablement », and « verité » were ubiquitous throughout the verse, verse-narrative, and prose.

After an introductory eulogy of Love and the All-Beautiful, the poet began a testimony to the All-Beautiful's true love as it had been related to him by an especial friend :

« Or vous diray, de point en point, / Si que je n'en mentiray point, / Tout ce que là me raconta. / Et ainsi dit, en son conte, a » (p. 4, lines 4-7). The four lines were a guarantee of the true reporting of the poet's especial friend's true reporting of an unknown lady's love, the truth of which was demonstrated by a *rondel*, which was likewise guaranteed by the poet as a true reporting of her true love : « Et pour ce que si noble chose / Ne doit celée estre n'enclose, / Vous diray, sans oster ne mettre, / Ce qu'il y avoit en la lettre » (p. 7, lines 11-14).

Here was a « voir dit » of a « voir dit » of a « voir dit », the composer of which was guaranteed to have « dit voir ». (Notwithstanding, the true report of Friend's words was octosyllabic, and contained one of the most contrived rich rhymes of the whole work — « raconta » : « conte a »). The tradition of eye-witness authentication and of second-hand reporting had reached sublimely ridiculous fruition even with these first « invraisemblances ».

Convinced by authentic, second-hand assertions that the unknown lady truly had spoken her love and had spoken truly, the poet then declared he now considered himself to have a lady : « si, que je tieng que j'ay amie / Belle, bonne, cointe et jolie » (p. 9, lines 18-19). This statement immediaiely became hypothesis, however, with a syntactic switch from its dogmatic present-tense assertion « je tieng » to a tentative conditional « bien porroie estre voir disans » (« *I could be speaking* truth »). An assertion of true love had been made, then undermined.

What *was* true was then introduced by « vraiment », but revised immediately with « voire » : « Car vraiement il a diz ans, / Voire, à m'entente, plus de douze, / Que j'ay goulousé et goulouse / Qu'Amours me donnast une dame » (lines 21-24). The truth was that the poet for ten years, no, truthfully, for more than twelve, had been in love with Love.

Convinced that the lady's worth, renown, beauty, sovereign sweetness, and kindness (all unproven) would not allow her to lie about true love, the true Annunciation of her favor to him now made him plead for a new Trinity — of Love, the Poet, and the Lady. « Or faisons une trinité / Et une amiable unité ; / Que ce soit uns corps et une ame, / D'Amours, de moy et de ma dame » (p. 10, lines 16-19). Such « true » love was not fact but faith. Belief was its substance and its substantiation ; *quod scit, loquitur, et quod (non) vidit, testatur.*

The record of love's Truth would be « nos escriptures » (p. 16, line 21) whose genesis and inspiration were the All-Beautiful. «Et s'il est nuls qui me repreingne, / Ou qui mal apaiez se teingne / De mettre cy nos escriptures, / ... Je respons a tous telement : / Que c'est au dous commandement / De ma dame qui le commande » (p. 16, lines 19 ff.).

In Truth's transmission the poet guaranteed there would be no lies (« jà n'i mentiray », p. 17, line 18). The truths of love would by definition encompass without distinction both the words and deeds of love. « Car celle pour qui Amours veille, / Vuet que je mete en ce VOIR-DIT / Tout ce qu'ay pour li *fait* et *dit*» (p. 17, lines 11-13).

Thus love-lyrics were as legitimately truth as was the narration of events. Indeed, lyrics *were* the main events of *Le Livre du Voir-dit*. The interpenetration of all words and deeds of love was symbolized in a chiasmus arrangement of « dire verité » and « faire loiauté » into « qui ne vorroit *dire (1)* ne *faire (2)* que *loiauté (2)* et *verité (1)* » (p. 20, line 7). Faithful and factual were there enmeshed.

The poet's love was sworn to be as true as fiction. It was guaranteed by fictional example. « Et si, vous jure et promet, que à mon povoir onques Lancelos n'aima Genevre, Paris Helaine, ne Tristan Yseult plus léaument que vous serez de moi amée et servie » (p. 21, lines 1-4). The juxtaposition of the inapposite « a mon povoir » to Lancelot's love (an area self-evidently beyond the poet's control, if not competence !) effectively nullified the « this-is-true » proposition once again.

The fiction of fables[5] was brought into conjunction with the facts of love, a Gorgon's head with the beloved's image, after the poet despaired at his dream of his beloved dressed in green. Love's anguish was attenuated by classical analogies, and the present was brought into perspective by a playful use of the past and of Ovid's *auctoritas* : « Ovides le dit en ses fables, / En moralitez *veritables*. / Se tels mutations véoies, / Certes moult t'en mervilleroies, / Quant de joie ainsi te desrobe / La mutation d'une robe » (p. 227, line 27 - p. 228, line 4).

The myth of Piquus (incorrectly rendered) was a « chose voire » (p. 287, line 21). The myth of Erichthonius (as it was told in a dream) was guaranteed true to the extent that Erichthonius was truly without a mother : « Et c'est voirs qu'elle (la créature) fu sans mère » (p. 322, line 12). The transformation of Lot's wife into a pillar of salt was « verité prouvée », confirmed by — Josephus ![6]

Like fables dreams were presented as both truth and as inconsequential aberration ; the poet sought for meaning in all dreams, yet his dreams played out the truth game in its most elaborate form. The sleeping poet played the game of « Truthful King » (« le Roi qui ne ment »), and in that game delivered a long statement about truth : « Belle chose est de verité / En bouche à roy, et grant vilté / De roy qui ha bouche qui ment » (p. 215, line 25 - p. 216, line 2). Truth was thus triple-mirrored by the poetic reporting of an imag-

---

[5] The unreliability of fable is asssumed in the series « ce n'estoit truffe ne songe, / *Fable*, contrueve, ne mensonge, / Ains falloit de nécessité / Qu'il en déissent verité» (p. 303, lines 29-32). Cf. also pp. 51-3 and 68 above.

[6] Paulin Paris claimed that Guillaume cited Josephus in preference to the Bible to avoid attributing the same authority to the Bible that he had granted to Ovid's *Metamorphoses* i.e. to pagan authority : « Machaut cite ici Josèphe de préférence à la Bible, pour ne pas être accusé d'accorder la même autorité aux livres saints et aux *Métamorphoses* d'Ovide » (p. 226, note 1). The explanation seems unlikely in view of Guillaume's fondness for mixing sacred and profane (see p. 75).

ined truth game which preached truth in a mendacious dream. « Car clerement vi que mon songe / N'avoit riens de vray fors mensonge » (p. 233, lines 4-5).

Traditional conventions from the lyric were both reinforced and contradicted when they were incorporated in *Le Livre du Voir-dit*. The poet's lady had requested *voir-dire* as she had previously requested the poet's love. The poet's truthfulness in *Le Livre du Voir-dit* became therefore a token of his obedience to love and of his disobedience to love's code of secrecy. Whenever the poet submissively assumed his conventional/unconventional lover's role, all previous love-traditions were simultaneously fulfilled and negated. An importunate lady had begged for love, an obedient lover had truthfully told their love to all and sundry : « vostre livre avera nom *Le Livre dou Voir dit* ; si, ne vueil ne ne doy mentir » (p. 263, lines 9-10).

The legal connotations of « voir-dire » provided added richness to an already complex lexicon. In the terminology of love the poet's truth-telling was « grant villenie » (p. 84, line 26), a judgment that the poet alternately accepted and rejected. In a legal context also the poet's truth-in-testifying was both « villenie » *and* vindication, his fictional/truthful testimony was both crime and cooperation. Because of his lady's authoritative « voir-dire » injunction to him, he must obediently offer testimony which was about to condemn him. « Car contre son commandement / Feroie du faire autrement : / Et, puisqu'il li plaist, il m'agrée, / S'obéiray à sa pensée » (p. 85, lines 2-5). Condemned by his own words he was also exonerated by them. Appropriately he commended himself truly to his lady « five hundred thousand times as often as lying — especially in love — had ever been perpetrated ». « Aussi, par .v.c. mille fois / Autant qu'on a menti de fois, / Dit mensonges et fait faus tours, / Especiaument en amours » (p. 365, lines 30-33).

The truthfulness of the lady also was doubted as often as it was asserted. Guillaume held truth in perpetual suspension by continually maintaining mutually exclusive propositions — a collection, as it were, of «she-loves-me» «she-loves-me-not» daisy-petals.

Significantly, it was Hope not Knowledge that guaranteed the lady's word. Hope's guarantees were tentative, with future-tense or hypothetical conditional verbs : « Et si t'a bien dit, cy devant, / Que tu dois estre tous séurs / Qu'elle t'aime, et c'est tes éurs / Qu'elle, pour riens ne le *diroit* / S'il n'estoit, et n'en *mentiroit*» (p. 88, lines 13-17); «et si, li as bien oÿ dire / Qu'elle vuet estre ton dous mire, / Et que jamais ne te laira ; / Et certes, jà n'en *mentira* » (*ibid.*, lines 24-27).

Hope, appearing variously as Espoirs or Esperance, could go unrecognized, however. « Et puet-estre que dites voir ; / Mais je vorroie bien savoir / Vostre nom ; si, m'escuseroie / Par devers vous, se je pooie » (p. 169, lines 5-8). Hope's guarantees of the lady's truth were counterbalanced by the poet's fearfulness and his misogyny, for which again he borrowed Ovid's authority. « Sed sunt diuersa puellis / Pectora »[7] became « Car c'est chose assez veritable, / Que trop est femme variable » (p. 333, lines 19-20). Yet even here Ovid's authoritative statement was undermined by Guillaume's impossible use of the adverb « assez » to modify the unmodifiable. The truth obviously became other than truth for being « *assez* veritable ».

Subsequently of course, the lady's variability was denied, when both she and the poet's priestly friend turned the accusation against the poet himself : « et pour ces .II. causes que j'ay devant dites, vous escri-je que vous estiez variables et que vous ne teniez pas bien verité » (p. 345, lines 22-24); «je vous di, sire, que, par m'ame, / Vous avez maniere de fame. / Trop souvent mue vos corages » (p. 355, lines 21-23). Inconstancy, the antithesis of true love, was Guillaume's constant attribute.

To Guillaume, then, the discourteous counsels of

[7]   *Ars amatoria*, ed. A.S. Hollis (Oxford, 1977), I, 755.

misogyny could be as convincing as the assurances of true love. And, like love's assurances, they too were guaranteed as true : « je le vous diray, / Ne jà ne vous en mentiray » (p. 284, lines 14-15); «Amis, par Dieu, c'est chose voire, / Qu'il a plus d'un asne à la foire » (p. 301, lines 21-2). The lover's world was constantly turned upside-down. Truth was synonymous with « villenie », reason with truth, love with a lie. Were lies then preferable to the truth ? Yes, since « souvent meschiet de dire voir » (p. 320, line 4).

This assertion of truth's disadvantages was not isolated. Having claimed truth for the whole work, Guillaume satirized the truth. The circumstances in which truth was told were frequently unworthy. The poet's « voir-dire » was in some ways reprehensible, so he blamed it on his lady. His secretary's veracity was based on fear : « et je savoie moult bien qu'il le / Me disoit veritablement, / Que faire n'osast autrement » (p. 114, lines 12-14).

Truth was unnecessary. « Mais, ce n'est pas necessité / Que quanqu'on dit soit verité » (p. 326, lines 17-18). Truth was dangerous. « Or en suis hors à deshonneur, / Et tout pour dire verité » (p. 320, lines 11-12). Truth was often ugly. « Tous voirs ne sont pas biaus à dire » (p. 319, line 20).

Truth guarantees were used by Guillaume in accordance with their tradition — they protested the truth of the inconsequential. The poet rode out for fresh air because, *in truth*, it was good for him : « Si m'en alay parmi les champs, / Pour oÿr des oisiaus les chans, / Et pour avoir l'air ; car *sans fable*, / Chose m'estoit moult profitable » (p. 43, lines 7-10). On the day of his lady's visit the poet said that *truly* he had never seen it rain so hard in all his life : « mais onques-mais ne vi pour *voir* / En ma vie si fort plouvoir » (p. 109, lines 8-9).

A truth guarantee served to introduce forty lines of inconsequential detail in which the poet had promised not to lie and which, indeed, he terminated to avoid lying : « pour ce un petit en parleray, / Ne jà le voir n'en celeray » (p. 82, lines 21-2). « Plus ne di de la grant richesse / De son habit, de sa noblesse, / Car bien dire ne le saroie, / Pour ce qu'espoir j'en mentiroie » (p. 84, lines 2-5).

Truth guarantees defended the *lieux communs* of love. *Truly* the lover never eats or drinks — he trembles, sweats, and faints for love : « Li las / Sera d'Amours si pris au las / Que ses corps tremblera de doubte, / Et si suera goute à goute ; / Il sera chaus et esméus, / Et de son goust si dechéus / Qu'il ne pourra mengier ne boire : / On le scet bien, *c'est chose voire* » (p. 34, lines 15-21).

Truth guarantees urged the literal acceptance of metaphor : « qu'*en verité*, / Mon cuer avés et m'amisté / Sans partir, en vo dous repaire » (p. 77, lines 14-16).

Truth guarantees preached the actual truth of hyperbole — the lady's real divinity and real miracles. « Et mis cuer et corps et estude, / Comment qu'il soient assez rude, / En ma douce dame honnourer.... Et, par Dieu, faire le devoie ... / Com à ma dame et ma déesse, / Et ma souveraine maistresse. / Car onques-mais je ne vi certes / Faire miracle si apertes / Com elle fist à ma personne ... Car *bien puis dire en verité* / Que .II. fois m'a ressuscité » (p. 31, line 29 - p. 32, line 11).

Truth guarantees were themselves undermined by unpredictable reversals: «Di-je chascuns? je ment, sans faille, / Car il n'est regle qui ne faille » (p. 171, lines 11-12). The juxtaposition of a hypothesis to a dogmatic assertion could render them impotent : « le quel *je reputay, sanz fable,* / Sage, loial et veritable, / Et *croy que pas ne se parjure* » (p. 250, lines 4-6) ; « car, *en verité, il m'estoit avis* qu'il avoit iii. ans que je n'avoie oÿ nouvelles de vous » (p. 344, line 1).

When truth's guarantee was explicitly modified to express hesitation concerning the truth, the subliminal message that had been flashing throughout the text became explicit. Then the poet in the fearful misogyny of creeping old age called his lady fickle Fortuna, and composed *Responses* to the latter questioning Her reliability. His refrain there challenged the title, themes, and motifs of *Le Livre du Voir-dit* by its « S'il est voirs ce qu'on m'en a dit ». Then it too disappeared, forgotten in the final accord of the « true » lovers.

Conclusion

The presence of formulae in medieval texts poses methodological problems to a modern scholar. All too frequently the recognition of a formula promotes a formulaic method of analysis. Stylistic usage is then neglected in favor of frequency of occurrence or variation in word-count and word-order. Sometimes the meaning and function of the formula are not examined. Consequently, many medieval formulae have been accepted on trust. Their literal content has remained unquestioned and they are assumed to serve their ostensible function.

Conventions serve a variety of functions, however. In the case of truth guarantees, a complex tradition of inherited presuppositions made paradox inevitable. The complexity of the tradition was not lessened when that paradox itself became traditional. When the assurance HERE-IS-TRUTH could be understood as equivocation or evasion, it no longer exploited the naïveté of a listening audience. In the age of Guillaume de Machaut conventions of truth engaged a highly sophisticated audience in a literary game.

Appendix One

GESTA GUILLELMI DUCIS NORMANNORUM
ET REGIS ANGLORUM —
A SUMMARY OF THE FACTS PRESENTED

At the death of Cnut his son Harold succeeded to the English throne. Edward and Alfred then were exiles in the Norman court. When Edward heard of Cnut's death, he attempted to invade England. He was defeated, and returned to Normandy. Soon after, Alfred, who was better prepared, landed in Canterbury. Godwin feigned welcome, but arranged for the capture of Alfred and some of his retainers whom he then sent to London. Harold had the men decapitated in front of Alfred. He sent Alfred bound and naked to a tortured exile on Ely. Alfred died of brain damage when his eyes were put out. At Harold's death his half-brother Harthacnut reigned briefly.

In Normandy William reached knighthood. Guy of Burgundy, Nigel of Cotentin, Rannulf of the Bessin, Haimo « Dentatus », and other magnates organized a revolt, and tried to overthrow him. A decisive battle was fought at Valès-Dunes with the help of King Henry of France. The enemy was routed. Guy was later captured at his stronghold in Brionne, and was pardoned. He returned to Burgundy. In return for Henry's assistance William joined him in the siege against Geoffrey Martel. At this period William was much respected by Henry. He was sought out also by Gascony, Auvergne, and even by the kings of Spain. Subsequently, Henry listened to evil slander by William's detractors, and conceived a great hatred for him. He then began his harassment of Normandy.

At Harthacnut's death Edward received Normandy's support in his bid for the English throne. Gratitude to William and to Normandy for their hospitality led him to arrange that William would inherit from him « rata donatione ». Peace had now been established in Normandy, but Geoffrey Martel was undermining William's influence outside the duchy in Anjou, Touraine, and Poitou. William attempted reprisals by invading Anjou to attack Domfront. In its vicinity he and fifty of his knights were nearly killed because of a treacherous informer. He turned and pursued his attackers intrepidly to the castle gates, even capturing a prisoner.

The siege of Domfront was difficult. Geoffrey Martel advanced to aid the besieged with a large army, but William learned his intentions through two scouts, Roger of Montgomery and William fitzOsborn. Geoffrey's army was obliged to flee, unsuccessful. William stormed Alençon, whose defeat terrified Domfront into submission. William then returned home.

He was advised by his barons of the necessity to marry. Kings from distant countries courted him as a future son-in-law, but it seemed preferable to contract an alliance with a neighboring power. William therefore allied himself with the dynasty of Baldwin, count of Flanders, by marrying Mathilda. After the wedding at Ponthieu, the couple led a triumphal procession to Rouen.

Opposition to William was forming again in Normandy and, after much insubordination, William of Arques resigned his vassalship. The duke placed a garrison in the stronghold of Arques, but it defected. William heard of the defection while in the Cotentin, and hastened to Arques. He met the reinforcements who had tried unsuccessfully to prevent Arques's provisioning. William attacked some of the count's men and drove them back inside the walls. Henry of France tried to bring help to Arques, but some of William's men ambushed and killed the French, including Enguerrand of Ponthieu. Hugh Bardoul was captured. Henry had to withdraw from his attempt to rescue the fortress, which William then starved into surrender.

William showed mercy to the count of Arques by allowing him to remain in the duchy. The coalition of Normans who had allied themselves with Henry (among them Guimond of Moulins and Guy of Poitiers) then fled. More violent unrest followed when Henry organized an all-out attack on Normandy, exploiting such causes of resentment as the death of Enguerrand of Ponthieu and the defeat of Geoffrey of Anjou. Burgundy, Auvergne, Gascony, France, and Brittanny all mobilized against Normandy.

Henry advanced through the Cotentin, reinforced by contingents from Aquitaine. Counts Odo and Rainald were to attack William's forces in « Gallia Belgica ». The bloody battle of Mortemer was a decisive victory for William. Odo and Rainald were surprised and defeated by the troops of Robert of Eu, Hugh of Gournay, Walter Giffard, William Crépin, and « other valiants ». Guy of Ponthieu was taken prisoner. King Henry was on the other side of the Seine. He decided to withdraw. A truce ended the various acts of hostility. Its terms were that William would hand back the French prisoners captured at Mortemer, and would retain in perpetuity the lands previously held by Geoffrey of Anjou.

William announced that he would fortify Ambrières, which was on the territory of Geoffrey of Mayenne (a vassal of Geoffrey Martel). The Normans then built the Ambrières stronghold. It was rumored that Geoffrey Martel was on his way to attack it, but, when there was no sign of him, William departed. Geoffrey then attacked, with the help of William of Aquitaine and Eudo of Penthièvre. William returned to the Ambrières siege, and the three counts and their armies fled.

Henry and Geoffrey Martel both attacked Normandy again. They traversed the Hiémois, and reached the Dives at the Varaville ford, where part of their army was cut off by the tide. It was slaughtered by William before the king's eyes. Henry never attacked Normandy again. At Henry's death the young Philip succeeded to the throne, and thenceforth there were good relations between the French and the Normans. Geoffrey Martel died.

William accepted the homage of Herbert of Maine and the right to inherit Herbert's territory. In return Herbert was to marry William's daughter. When Herbert died of an illness and, contrary to arrangement, Walter of Mantes was declared Herbert's heir, William began a long harassment of the region. After he had overthrown all the strongholds in Le Mans, the inhabitants of the *comté* did him deference with feigned pleasure. William now had virtual mastery over Maine. William brought Herbert's sister Marguerite to be his son Robert's bride (she died before the marriage). William stormed a castle owned by Geoffrey of Mayenne.

Edward the Confessor sent Harold to William to confirm William's future succession to the English throne. Harold was captured *en route* by Guy of Ponthieu, and was imprisoned. William hastened to demand Harold's safety. Guy took Harold to Eu then, and was rewarded for his cooperation with land and wealth. William hospitably welcomed Harold at Rouen. Harold swore an oath of fealty to William concerning the English succession.

Conan of Britanny was now in revolt against Normandy, and William built the castle of St. James in the Avranchin as a check to Conan's power. Conan besieged Dol, held by William's Celtic ally Rhiwallon, but he fled at William's arrival. William did not pursue him far. He intended in fact to leave Brittanny, but Conan allied himself with Geoffrey of Anjou. William waited to contend with them both. He was victorious. Rhiwallon's constant complaint that invasion was invasion from whatever quarter made William forbid plunder and pillage in Rhiwallon's territory.

Harold returned home after the Breton campaign with gifts and with his nephew Hakon (previously William's hostage). William ruled Normandy strictly, repressing revolt and rapine, enforcing the laws, rewarding orthodoxy, and endowing ecclesiastical establishments. He conversed with ecclesiastics of good repute, and especially loved and respected Lanfranc. He deposed Mauger from the archbishopric of Rouen for unseemly behavior, and appointed Maurilius in his place. Gerbert was appointed head of the monastery of St. Wandrille. Hugh was nominated to Lisieux, Odo to Bayeux, and John to Avranches. Two Spanish suitors sought to marry William's daughter, and foreign visitors courted his favor. All Normandy was fearful when William came close to death through an illness.

News arrived of Edward's death and of Harold's seizure of the English throne. William made provisions for a prolonged absence from Normandy, and began preparations for a fleet. While the fleet waited in the Dives, William provided for fifty thousand soldiers without recourse to pillage. He asked the blessing of Pope Alexander II for his undertaking, and received a papal banner. He had already made alliances with Emperor Henry IV and with Sweyn, King of Denmark. Harold also was making extensive preparations.

William moved his fleet to St. Valéry, hiding from his men the losses and accidents that had been sustained in the crossing, and encouraging the faltering. When a favorable wind at last arrived, the fleet moved rapidly. William's ship had a light at its mast-head so that the other ships could cluster around it that night, but it was so fast that it lost the others. William reassured his men by dining calmly. Eventually the rest of the fleet found William's ship.

Disembarkation took place at Pevensey without any struggle, because Harold had traveled north to defend the kingdom against Tosti and Harold Hardrada. The Normans fortified Pevensey, then Hastings. William scouted the territory in person, accompanied by only twenty-five knights. A powerful Norman who had settled in the area, Robert, son of Lady Guimara, warned William to withdraw. William answered that he would be desirous of combat even if he had only ten thousand and not sixty thousand men. A monk-ambassador of Harold's cautioned the Normans to withdraw. (William received the message first in person by pretending to be his own seneschal). William responded with a statement of his legitimate claims to the English throne. He offered Harold a duel. Harold responded by invoking the judgment of God.

At the news of the king's approach William took Mass, and prayed with the army. Odo of Bayeux, Geoffrey of Coutances, and many monks and clergy were present. William scorned the « sinistra conversio » of his cuirass. He arranged the army so that foot-soldiers with bows and arrows were in front, foot-soldiers with both bows and cuirass were behind them, and the cavalry was in the rear. Harold's soldiers chose the tactical advantage of a hill, and they took their stand on foot. The duke and his men began to climb the steep slopes, and the Normans engaged battle.

The ferocity of the English response and their great tactical advantage discouraged William's men. The infantry, the Breton knights, and the left wing of the auxiliaries retreated, then the whole army fled back. A demoralizing rumor that William was dead began to circulate in the army. William saw the English beginning to pursue, he rallied his men, and took off his helmet to demonstrate that he was alive. Then the Normans began to surround the vulnerable little group of pursuers.

William attacked again. The solidly-massed English resisted strongly. Individual Normans already had begun to make breaches in the English mass, however. Others from Maine, France, and Aquitaine followed them, the Normans always fighting with exceptional valor. Robert of Beaumont distinguished himself as leader of the right-wing battalion. The Normans and their allies then resorted to « feigned flight », having seen its success previously. Wheeling around in mid-retreat, they massacred their pursuers to a man.

William then attacked with a number of diverse tactics, and the English weakened under a rain of arrows. They finally fled, pursued by the Normans. Isolated English continued their fighting from ditches. Eustace of Boulogne was wounded while he was predicting William's death. William surveyed the battlefield. Harold's body was unrecognizable except for certain hidden marks of identity. William handed over the body to William Malet for burial, refusing the offer made by Harold's mother to pay for its weight in gold. He placed a garrison at Hastings under Humphrey of Tilleul, then savagely punished Romney for having attacked some of his men. He marched to Dover, which surrendered in fear despite its natural advantages. William was lenient, helping its inhabitants rebuild what had been burned in the siege of their city. Dysentery attacked the army.

Canterbury offered its submission to William even before he arrived there. William took up quarters at the « Broken Tower ». He was stricken with dysentery. Stigand, Edwin, and Morcar were meanwhile trying to establish Edgar the Atheling as king. William moved towards London, despatching five hundred Norman knights ahead of him, and forcing the opposition to take refuge within the walls. William's men inflicted carnage and destruction by fire on the south side. William marched across the Thames to Wallingford. Stigand reversed himself and did homage to William, thus renouncing allegiance to Edgar the Atheling. William marched directly on London. The bishops and nobles requested that he be their king. William displayed some hesitation, and submitted the request to his leaders for their advice. Aimeri of Thouars was the most vocal in his persuasion. William hastened to have London fortified and, since there was no resistance to his plans, hunted falcon until the time of his coronation.

William was presented to the English by Aldred, Archbishop of York, and to the French by Bishop Geoffrey of Coutances. He was crowned in St. Peter's Basilica, Westminster Abbey, on Christmas Day, 1066. (Stigand had been anathematized by the Pope). An accident occurred when William's armed guards around the Abbey mistook the acclamation for rioting, and set fire to the neighborhood with the intention of allowing William to escape.

As King of England, William showed beneficence to all supporters, to monasteries, to St. Peter's in Rome, and to churches in France, Aquitaine, Auvergne, and, of course, Normandy. English towns and wealthy magnates who had opposed him redeemed themselves by paying tribute. After the coronation the king moved out of London, and stayed some days in Barking while London was being fortified. He received the submission of Edwin, Morcar, and Copsige of Northumbria. They were reinstated and honored. William traveled over the country, restoring confiscated territory, hearing supplications, receiving gifts, fortifying strongholds with reliable allies, and distributing fiefs. Recognizing the strategic position of Guenta, he fortified it, and left William fitzOsborn in control of the northern region there. His brother Odo, bishop of Bayeux, was given Dover and made Earl of Kent. William then sailed to Normandy from Pevensey, accompanied by Stigand, Edgar the Atheling, Edwin, Morcar, and Walthof.

All Normans returning to Normandy were liberally rewarded for their services. William was joyfully welcomed back, and gave many gifts to Norman churches. Normandy had been well governed in his absence by Mathilda and by Roger of Beaumont because of the respect felt for William even in his absence. The new king celebrated Easter at Fécamp, and entertained a dazzling court of Normans, visitors, and captive English at the feast. He spent the Summer, Autumn and part of the Winter in Normandy, living in moderation and prohibiting pillage. Meanwhile, however, various areas of subjugated England were secretly negotiating with the Danes. Some English went into exile, intending to return with foreign soldiers. Eustace of Boulogne switched allegiance by supporting the inhabitants of Kent in their revolt. Despite a surprise nocturnal attack on Dover castle while Odo of Bayeux and Hugh of Montfort were on the other side of the Thames, that garrison withstood capture, Eustace's nephew was taken prisoner, and Eustace fled back across the Channel. Around the same time Copsige was ambushed and murdered. Ealdred, archbishop of York ...

(The *Gesta Guillelmi* lacks both introduction and conclusion.)

Appendix Two

GESTA FRANCORUM
ET ALIORUM HIEROSOLIMITANORUM —
A SUMMARY OF THE FACTS PRESENTED

There was a strong movement throughout France to enlist for a crusade to the Holy Land. It was promoted by the exhortation of Urban II, and there were three main groups of Crusaders. One group (with Peter the Hermit, duke Godfrey, Baldwin his brother, and Baldwin of Mons) entered Hungary, and followed « Charlemagne's route » to Constantinople. Peter arrived there first on July 30 with most of the Germans. The Longobards were already there, as were many others. The Crusaders were granted permission to reprovision, but they plundered and devastated with such excess that Alexius ordered them across the Bosphorus. All along the route they continued their devastation.

At Nicomedia the Longobards and Germans separated from the Franks because of Frankish arrogance. The Longobards elected a leader (Rainald). The Germans did the same. The Turks besieged the Crusaders at Exergorgo. The Christians suffered agonies of thirst for eight days. The German leader abandoned camp, pretending that he was about to attack the enemy. Many Christians were massacred there. The Turks then destroyed many of the troops of Peter the Hermit and Walter the Penniless at Civitot. The emperor was delighted that the Christians were dispersed and in such disarray. He had them rounded up and brought across the Bosphorus. These events took place in October.

The second group of Crusaders entered Esclavonia with Raimond of St.-Gilles and the bishop of Puy.

The third group (with Bohemond, Richard « de Princi
patu », Robert of Flanders, Robert of Normandy, Hugh
Magnus, Evrard of Puiset, Achard of Montmerle, and
Isuard of Mouzon) took the old Roman route, leaving from
Brindisi, Bari or Otranto. The governor of Durazzo waylaid
Hugh and William, the marquis' son, inducing them to
swear allegiance to the emperor.

Godfrey was the first of the leaders to arrive in Constantinople, on December 23. His camp was attacked by Turcopoli and Pincinati on the emperor's orders. The duke's
brother, Baldwin, ambushed the attackers, killing and
capturing many. The duke moved quarters outside the city,
the emperor attacked, and the duke repulsed the attack. An
agreement was signed allowing the army to reprovision in
Constantinople, and providing a subvention for the destitute, after which the army would cross the Bosphorus.

At the siege of Amalfi du Pont-Scaphard Bohemond
took the cross, and Count Roger's men flocked to join him.
He returned home to prepare, then he and his army crossed
the sea to « Bulgaria ». They gathered in the rich valley of
Andronopolis. Traveling from city to city, they arrived at
Castoria on December 25, then at Pelagonia, where they
attacked and burned the heretics. At the river Vardar Bohemond continued on, while the count of Russignol and his
brothers remained. They were attacked by the emperor.
Tancred and two thousand others retraced their steps to join
battle with the Turcopoli and Pincinati on February 18.
They were victorious and took prisoners, whom Bohemond
later freed. The emperor gave the army an escort to super-
vise their provisioning. Bohemond forbade the pillage of
Christian territory, which caused a grave dispute with Tancred and others.

The army encamped at Serra, and Bohemond ordered
them to give back all plundered cattle. They arrived at Rusa,
where the Greeks came out to meet them. They pitched
camp there on April 1. Bohemond went on to Constantinople to speak with the emperor. Tancred remained at the

head of the army, leading them to a fertile valley where they celebrated Easter.

The emperor lodged Bohemond outside Constantinople and requested a secret conference — Godfrey and his brother were present also. A Constantinople council of dignitaries decided that the Crusaders should swear fealty to the emperor. The Crusaders refused. Raimond of St.-Gilles was now near the city also. The emperor made an agreement with Bohemond, giving him land beyond Antioch in return for his oath, and promising him safe conduct.

Raimond of St.-Gilles lodged outside Constantinople, and the emperor asked for his homage and fealty. However, Raimond wanted revenge on the imperial army. The Crusading leaders remonstrated with him, and he finally swore to the emperor a limited oath which did not include homage. Bohemond's army was now near Constantinople. To avoid the oath Tancred and Richard « de Principatu », with almost all of Bohemond's army, secretly crossed the Bosphorus. Raimond's army then arrived at Constantinople where he and they remained. Bohemond also remained at Constantinople to arrange for the provisioning of the troops beyond Nicaea. Godfrey went to Nicomedia with Tancred and the others. They remained three days.

The duke sent three thousand men with axes and swords to widen the route to Nicaea. They marked the route with crosses mounted on stakes. Thus the army came to Nicaea on May 6 and pitched camp. Until Bohemond arrived with arrangements for provisioning by sea, the hungry army was buying bread at 20 or 30 *denarii*. The army began the siege of Nicaea on May 14. On May 16 Raimond of St.-Gilles and the bishop of Puy seized the south gate by which the Turks were expecting to receive reinforcements. The army mined a tower, but the Turks restored it the same night. The leaders and their men cooperated in a blockade of the front of the city. (The Turks were still able to provision from the lake side). The Crusading leaders sent for the emperor's help, and he sent his Turcopoli. The Turks then capitulated to the emperor, who received them well, intending to use them against the Franks. The siege of Nicaea had lasted seven weeks and three days.

The emperor rewarded the Crusaders with rich gifts to the poor among them. They left Constantinople, encamped two days at a bridge, left before dawn, and fell into two groups. Bohemond, Robert of Normandy, and Tancred were in the first ; Raimond of St.-Gilles, Godfrey, the bishop of Puy, Hugh Magnus, and the count of Flanders were in the second. The Turks made a violent attack on the first group. They were repulsed by Bohemond and his army (the camp women brought water to the defenders, and gave them constant encouragement).

Bohemond sent urgent messages to the rest of the army. Godfrey, Hugh Magnus, the bishop of Puy, and Raimond of St.-Gilles soon arrived. The Crusading army was then drawn up with Bohemond, Robert of Normandy, Tancred, Robert of Ansa, and Richard « de Principatu » on the left. The bishop of Puy was to approach from another direction so that the Turks would be surrounded. Godfrey, the count of Flanders, and Hugh Magnus were on the right wing. When the Crusaders approached, the host of Turks, Arabs, Saracens, Angulans, and other barbarians fled. For a whole day the Christians pursued and killed them. They won much booty. Godfrey of Monte-Scabioso and William the marquis' son were among those killed.

The Christians continued to pursue the Turks from place to place, through deserts and uninhabitable land, until they arrived at Iconium and Heraclea. There a large troop of Turks was waiting. The Christians attacked and defeated them. The Turks fled and left the city to the Christians. The army remained there for four days. Tancred and Baldwin left for the valley of Botenthrot. Tancred went on to Tarsus and repulsed the Turks when they came out of the city to meet him. He and his army camped outside Tarsus. Baldwin then arrived and wanted to sack the city. Tancred refused because the city was Christian, but his army was smaller than Baldwin's, and he was obliged to leave Tarsus. He took possession of Adana and Manustra.

The large army, with Raimond de St.-Gilles, Bohemond, and Godfrey entered Armenia, authorized several strongholds to be held in the name of the Crusade and the emperor, then crossed from Caesarea to Cappadocia, then to Coxon. The Christian inhabitants handed the latter over at once, and the army stayed there three days. Raimond of St.-Gilles decided to occupy Antioch, and sent Peter of Castillon, William of Montpellier, Peter of Roaix, Pierre-Raimond d'Hautpoul, and five hundred knights ahead of him. Peter of Roaix made various minor attacks and conquests, among them Rusa.

That part of the army which had stayed in Coxon was now obliged to cross treacherous mountains to reach Marasch. Many knights sold their armor because of its impossible weight. They were welcomed at Marasch. They reprovisioned with gifts from Marasch, then traveled on to the valley of Antioch. As they approached the Iron Bridge their scouts were blocked by a party of Turks who were hastening to the rescue of Antioch. The Christians put the Turks to flight, killed some, and won horses, camels, mules, and loaded asses. The army arrived and camped on the river-bank. Bohemond began the siege on October 21 with four thousand knights. Only three gates were accessible — a mountain protected the fourth side, allowing only limited access. The army found abundance in the fertile area where they were camped.

The Turks inside the city did not respond for fifteen days. They were ascertaining the army's movements through Armenian and Syrian spies. Then the Turks began sorties. Those stationed in the Aregh stronghold were particularly troublesome, and Bohemond's troop became involved in a mêlée with them. Two Christians were killed.

The Christians decided to protect themselves with a fortification on Mt. Maregart. The leaders guarded it by turns. Before Christmas supplies were already dwindling. Since it was not safe to forrage in small groups, the army arranged a division of labor : one group would take charge of the defence while the other was seeking provisions. On the Monday after Christmas, therefore, Bohemond and the count of Flanders left for Saracen territory with twenty thousand knights and foot-soldiers. Turks, Arabs, and Saracens from Jerusalem, Damascus, and Aleppo, who were massing to help Antioch tried unsuccessfully to drive the forragers from the territory.

The Turks in Antioch took advantage of the absence of Bohemond and the count to attack their besiegers. There were many losses. Meanwhile Bohemond and his men went as far as « Tancred's Stronghold » to forrage. They had no success, and the Armenians and Syrians profited from their failure by selling food at exorbitant prices to the hungry army.

William the Carpenter and Peter the Hermit tried to escape, were recaptured by Tancred, and were brought back in humiliation. The Franks interceded with Bohemond on William's behalf, but subsequently he fled again. Tatikios abandoned the Crusaders, promising to bring back supplies. The Crusaders were now tortured by famine, and were hard-pressed on all sides by the Turks. The destitute were fleeing to Cyprus, Romania, and the mountains. There was no means of reaching the sea for fear of the Turks.

Bohemond heard that a large Turkish army was approaching, and held a council of war. He spent a night between the river and the lake, then sent scouts to investigate the enemy's movements. The scouts reported the arrival of a large bi-partite Turkish army. Bohemond drew up six battalions : five to attack the enemy and his own battalion to bring up the rear. After initial hand-to-hand combat, the whole enemy army arrived to drive back the Crusaders. Bohemond sent Robert, son of Gerard, for the banner, around which the Crusaders rallied. They then attacked with such energy that the Turks were driven right to the Far Bridge. Many were killed by Armenians or Syrians. The

Crusaders won horses and many necessaries from the enemy. They carried one hundred heads to the quarters of the Babylon emir's ambassadors. Their rout of the Turks took place on February 9. (Back in camp the army had fought all day at three of the city's gates.)

The leaders held a council and decided to build a stronghold at the Machumaria, situated at the city's harbor-gate. Raimond of St.-Gilles and Bohemond went to Port-St.-Simeon to find men for the task. The army had just begun to build the stronghold when the Turks attacked them. They fled, and several were killed. The next day the Turks prepared an ambush for those returning from the port. Only those who fled quickly escaped death. More than one thousand knights and footsoldiers were massacred that day.

Bohemond followed a different route to the camp, and furiously engaged combat with the Turks, who fled across the bridge into the city. Many were drowned. Fighting continued until nightfall. Twelve emirs and fifteen hundred Turks died. When the Turks inside the city came out next day to bury their dead, the army dragged the corpses out from the ground and executed them. They then tallied the heads, except for those they had sent to the sea on four horses that belonged to the emir's ambassadors.

On the third day the army began again to build their stronghold, this time from stones taken from Turkish tombs. After the construction was finished, the army was able to harass the enemy on all sides. Now only the river exit remained open to the Turks. The army took council, and Tancred agreed for four hundred silver marks to occupy the stronghold on the river. Tancred then captured the Armenians and Syrians who were bringing supplies to the Turks, thus blocking Turkish access to the outside world.

A Crusading council promised Bohemond the city if he could capture it. Bohemond called for the help of his ally Firouz, a Turkish emir, against the approaching army of Turks, Publicans, Azymites, and others. He summoned the Frankish army, and they rode and marched until dawn.

They scaled the walls of the city on June 3. Iagi Sian and others were killed in flight.

Kerboga assembled an army of Turks, Saracens, Publicans, Azymites, Kurds, Persians, Angulans, and others to dispel the Franks from Antioch. On June 6 the pagan army camped between the two rivers, and remained there two days. Kerboga was given the defence of the citadel by Schems ed daula, and the Franks were so hard-pressed that William of Grandmesnil and his brother Alberic, Guy Trousseau, and Lambert the Pauper fled.

Three Crusaders were blocked in a tower in front of the citadel, two fled, but the third defended himself with valor. Bohemond could not find men who were willing to fight in the vicinity of the citadel, and ordered a fire to be started therefore on the side of the city that contained Iagi-Sian's palace. A wind arose, and two thousand churches and habitations burned. The Turks in the citadel continued to fight day and night.

The Crusaders were suffering grievously from famine. Stephen, count of Chartres, feigned illness to desert to Alexandreta. Later, fearful at the sight of the many tents near Antioch, he fled to the emperor at Philomena. He reported that Antioch had been captured and that the Crusaders were about to be exterminated. He advised the emperor to go back to Constantinople with his army. Bohemond's despairing brother Guy questioned Stephen's integrity. The emperor ordered the countryside of Bulgaria to be razed against a Turkish advance, then returned to Constantinople. Crusaders who were too weak to follow the army died.

The leaders sent envoys, among them Peter the Hermit and Herlouin, to warn Kerboga out of Christian territory. The message was rejected. The army continued to endure fear and famine. After three days of fasting, penance, and masses according to the two rites, six battle corps were set up under Hugh Magnus and the count of Flanders, Godfrey, Robert of Normandy, the bishop of Puy (with the

Holy Lance), Tancred, and Bohemond. They went out by the Machumarian Gate, and Kerboga withdrew towards the mountains when he saw their numbers. The Turks then formed two divisions, one to go to the sea side, the other to attack the Crusaders. The Crusaders divided also.

A seventh battle corps was formed from the troops of Bohemond and the count of Normandy. Rainald led it towards the Turks from the sea side. The Turks engaged combat, but could not withstand the Crusaders. They lit a fire (their pre-arranged signal of defeat), then they and all who saw the fire fled. The Crusaders attacked, conquered, and pursued as far as the Far Bridge, then even further to « Tancred's Stronghold ». The Turks abandoned everything, and were killed as they fled by Armenians and Syrians who blocked the path to the mountains. The emir requested a truce and treaty with Bohemond : pagans who converted would remain, all others would be permitted to leave in safety. Bohemond agreed and placed men in the citadel. The emir was baptized together with many others. Bohemond had the rest escorted to Saracen territory. This battle took place on June 28.

The leaders sent Hugh Magnus to bring the emperor to receive Antioch, but Hugh failed to return. The council decided that the Crusading pilgrimage would have to be postponed until early November, because Syria was too arid to be crossed in Summer. The leaders dispersed. They had guaranteed support to those who needed it in the waiting period.

Raimond Pilet and his army ventured into Saracen territory, captured Tell-Mannas and a neighboring stronghold, and converted or killed the peasants of the area. They returned briefly to Tell-Mannas, then made a sortie to nearby Marra. In Marra Turks and Saracens from Aleppo and all the surrounding cities were assembled. They attacked the Crusaders and temporarily put them to flight.

A full day's fighting in the heat gave the Crusaders no advantage. The Syrians and the footsoldiers panicked, and in their retreat many Christians were massacred by the pursuing Turks (July 5). Those who escaped returned to their stronghold where Raimond Pilet remained for some time with his army. At Antioch the bishop of Puy died.

Raimond of St.-Gilles took possession of El-Bâra, Christianized it, and had a bishop appointed. The leaders returned to Antioch in November to discuss the continuation of the Crusade. Bohemond and Raimond of St.-Gilles were in disagreement over the possession of Antioch. Bohemond recited the terms of the agreement that had been made to him, and Raimond cited the agreement *he* had made with the emperor. Eventually Raimond declared himself willing to abide by the terms of the leaders' agreement except insofar as they might infringe upon his own allegiance to the emperor. Bohemond then took council for the long-term defence of Antioch's citadel, and Raimond did likewise for the palace of Iagi-Sian and the Port-St.-Simeon Gate.

Raimond and his men left Antioch and traveled via Rugia and Albara to Marra, which they reached and attacked on November 26. They then prepared for siege, and Marra was captured on December 11. The Franks stayed there one month and four days. The bishop of Orange died at Marra.

The discord between Bohemond and Raimond of St.-Gilles continued. Despite another leaders' council, their differences over Antioch could not be reconciled. Finally Bohemond and the leaders returned to Antioch, and Raimond returned to Marra to fortify the palace and the St.-Simeon Gate. On January 13 he left Marra barefoot to resume the pilgrim route. He stayed three days at Capharda where the count of Normandy joined him. The other Crusading group took up quarters near Caesarea on the Farfar. The king of Caesarea became anxious when he saw the Franks encamped so near, and he sent two Turks to guide them to better hunting-grounds. They occupied various strongholds, among them Kephalia, and received various agreements of submission including that of the king of Tripolis.

Raimond Pilet and Raimond of Turena left Raimond of St.-Gilles's army, and captured Tortosa. Godfrey, Bohemond, and the count of Flanders traveled to Laodicea, and while they besieged Gibellum, Bohemond returned to Antioch. The army made peace with the emir and joined forces with Raimond of St.-Gilles against the possible approach of the pagans (who did not, however, arrive). The counts took part in the siege of Arca, which lasted three months and a day.

A successful attack was made on Tripolis, and forraging was done beyond the Sem. Godfrey, Raimond of St.-Gilles, and Raimond of Flanders made an agreement with the king of Tripolis to leave the siege of Arca and go to Jerusalem. Traveling via Bethelon, Zebari, Beyrouth, Sidon, Tyre, Acre, and Haifa, they celebrated Pentecost on May 29 near Caesarea, appointed a bishop for St. George's outside Ramola, and reached Jerusalem on Tuesday, June 7.

The leaders besieged Jerusalem from various sides. The army was beset by a shortage of water and provisions. During the siege they received a call for help from their ships in the port of Haifa, and sent one hundred men from Raimond of St.-Gilles's army. Thirty of them became separated from the others, and got into a mêlée with seven hundred Arabs, Turks, and Saracens from the emir's army. Achard of Montmerle and some poor footsoldiers were killed, but the rest rallied, attacked, and even managed to plunder one hundred and three horses.

The army built siege-machines, and made several unsuccessful assaults on Jerusalem. On July 15 the emir in the Tower of David opened the gate and the Crusaders entered. Massacring, they pursued the Saracens right to Solomon's Temple. Raimond of St.-Gilles arranged the safe escort of the emir and his entourage to Ascalon. On July 22 after prayer and fasting they elected Godfrey prince of the city, and on August 1 Arnulph was elected Patriarch.

Tancred and Count Eustace were invited to receive Neapolis. Thence they proceeded in the direction of Ascalon on Bohemond's orders, since a Saracen attack was being prepared against the Franks in that city. Tancred gathered information about the enemy's plans from Arab scouts, and sent for the help of Godfrey, the Patriarch, and the leaders in Jerusalem. The duke, the Patriarch, and Robert of Flanders left on August 9 with the bishop of Martorano. Raimond of St.-Gilles and Robert of Normandy would not consent to the journey unless the news of an attack were confirmed.

The Patriarch, the bishop, and the various nobles congregated on the river-bank near Ascalon, and the army plundered many animals. They pursued three hundred Arabs. That evening the Patriarch forbade plunder until after the battle. The next day at dawn the leaders ordered their men ready for battle, with Godfrey on the left, Raimond of St.-Gilles on the right, the counts of Normandy and Flanders, Tancred, and all the others in the center. Robert of Normandy attacked the emir's standard, the count of Flanders attacked the pagans, and Tancred ventured into the pagan camp. The pagans fled, and the emir's standard was picked up and sold to Robert of Normandy, who donated it to the Patriarch. After the battle there was much plundering and burning. This battle took place on August 12.

Appendix Three

In 1198 Fulk of Neuilly began preaching the Crusade. By
the authority of Pope Innocent an indulgence was granted
to all who enlisted. In the next two years many took the
Cross, and the leaders held frequent parliaments. Eventually at Soissons they appointed six envoys with plenary
powers who approached the doge of Venice requesting aid.
A treaty was signed in April 1201 by which Venice would
provide transports for four thousand five hundred horse
and nine thousand squires, ships with four thousand five
hundred knights and twenty thousand foot-soldiers, and
also provisions for nine months. Fifty armed galleys would
be added free on condition that Venice received half of all
conquests. The total cost would be ninety-four thousand
marks, and the duration of the agreement would be one
year. The messengers borrowed two thousand marks to
make the down-payment for the fleet.

In June 1201 the leaders elected Boniface of Montferrat
to head the expedition. In June 1202 the Crusaders began to
assemble in Venice. Unfortunately, because of defections to
other ports, the leaders could not get together enough
money to meet their obligations. Despite loans, a second
collection from the whole army, then a second collection
from certain barons, they still needed thirty-four thousand
marks. The doge suggested that the Crusaders help Venice
reconquer Zara, and Venice then would waive its demands
for the remainder of the money until it could be won by con-

quest. This was agreed upon, and, as September approached, the barons began to take delivery of the ships.

At that time Alexius, nephew of the emperor of Constantinople, was on his way to Philip of Swabia. He met numbers of Crusaders en route, and his advisers suggested he ask them for help in his attempt to claim the throne. The Crusaders agreed to help Alexius on condition that he provide help to their expedition. The Crusading fleet set sail for Zara in the octave of St.-Rémi, 1202, with more than three hundred petraries, mangonels, and siege-weapons. They arrived on the eve of St.-Martin, and the next day captured the port, broke its protective chain, and landed. There was a faction in the army that disapproved of the siege of Zara — their spokesman was a Cistercian abbé from Vaux-de-Cernay. The siege of Zara lasted a good five days, then Zara surrendered to the doge.

The army decided to winter there, the Venetians on the seaward side, the Franks on the other. On the third day there was violent fighting between Crusaders and Venetians. In January messengers arrived from Germany with Alexius' proposal that in return for their help to him he would provide two hundred thousand silver marks, provisions for the army, his own service for one year together with ten thousand men, and five hundred men to be maintained overseas at his expense for the rest of his life. Constantinople would be restored to Roman obedience. The abbé of Vaux-de-Cernay led the opposition, but the agreement was signed. Alexius would arrive fifteen days after Easter.

Defections continued through the winter. The leaders sent envoys to the Pope, who absolved them for their attack upon Christian Zara. Before leaving Zara the Venetians destroyed its walls and towers. The army set out for Corfu, Alexius arrived from Constantinople, and the Crusaders all finally sailed for Durazzo, then for Corfu. They stayed there three weeks, then left on the eve of Pentecost, 1203, for Scutari, making various stops en route. They stayed at Scutari nine days. Alexius sent a message by Nicholas Rosso asking the reason for this invasion of his territory. Conon de Béthune responded for the barons that the territory was not rightfully the emperor's, but should be restored to Alexius, son of his brother. The next day the doge, the marquis and Alexius sailed under the walls of the city to show Alexius to the people. There was no response.

The Crusaders planned battle strategy for seven battalions and, on the appointed day, the army moved, with each galley towing a transport. The port was captured without resistance. They plundered the emperor's tents, and encamped in the Jewish quarter of Estanor, in front of the Galata tower. They captured the latter the next day. The siege of the city from land and sea began on July 10, and lasted until July 18.(The Crusaders were outnumbered two hundred to one.) The emperor fled, and the inhabitants reinstated Isaac, who was crowned on August 1, 1203.

The leaders visited Isaac to confirm Alexius' agreement. Isaac hesitated over the promised terms, but eventually agreed. The Crusaders restored Alexius to his father. Towards the projected time of the Crusaders' departure, the emperor begged them to defer their departure until March, when he hoped to be able to pay them. They agreed to stay for a further year from Michaelmas.

By the advice of the Greeks and French, Alexius left Constantinople with many of the barons to subdue his territories. All did fealty and homage except John of Wallachia. Meanwhile a mêlée arose between the Greeks and Latins in Constantinople, resulting in a disastrous two-day fire. Regugees fled in boats to the Crusaders' encampment.

Alexius and the barons returned to Constantinople on November 11. Payments to the army dwindled and eventually stopped. Boniface reproached the emperor, then the barons sent an ultimatum and challenge. Thus war began again and lasted through the winter. Once the Greeks sent seventeen fire-ships into the fleet, but the Venetians immediately dragged them into the straits. Mourzuphles and the Greeks plotted to capture and imprison Alexius. Mourzuphles was crowned emperor, Isaac died, and Mourzuphles had Alexius poisoned, strangled, then buried with pomp and ceremony. The clergy then maintained that the war against the Greeks was just, and that if the Crusaders restored Greece to the Roman rite, they would be absolved for their attacks upon Constantinople.

Now there were skirmishes by land or sea almost every day. (Those who went to other ports — and they numbered more than those at Constantinople — achieved nothing). Preparations, especially of war-machines, continued on both sides. The Crusaders arranged terms for distribution of fiefs and booty if Constantinople were captured. On the Thursday after mid-Lent the fleet set sail against the city. They attacked in more than one hundred places, but were repulsed. After two days of repair they returned, the scaling-ships bound together two by two. The *Paradise* and the *Pilgrim* joined on to a tower, then four towers were captured, three gates entered, and the knights rode to Mourzuphle's tents. Mourzuphle fled that night. Constantinople was captured on April 12, 1204.

The booty from Constantinople was distributed (although some kept what they had taken), and the Venetians were paid fifty thousand silver marks. After much discord over the two rivals, Baldwin of Flanders and Boniface of Montferrat, twelve chosen electors elected Baldwin Emperor of Romania. Before the coronation Boniface of Montferrat married the empress who had been Isaac's wife. Baldwin was crowned on May 16, 1204. Boniface asked Baldwin for Salonika (which was near the kingdom of his wife's brother, the king of Hungary) instead of the territory that had been promised him on the other side of the straits near Turkey. Salonika was granted to him.

Mourzuphles was only four days' journey from Constantinople at Messinopolis. When he sacked Tchorlu, Baldwin decided after council with the leaders to make a campaign of conquest through the territory. Meanwhile by treachery Alexius had Mourzuphles blinded. Baldwin moved from Constantinople to Adrianople, and left a garrison there. He progressed to Messinopolis, but Alexius had fled. Boniface also encamped at Messinopolis, and urged Baldwin not to march in the direction of Salonika. Baldwin insisted that he would, and the resulting discord threatened all that the expedition had so far achieved.

Baldwin rode to Salonika, capturing Blache and Cetros on the way. He remained three days encamped in front of the city. Boniface also rode back, capturing Demotika and winning much Greek support around his territories. After much contention Baldwin and Boniface were reconciled, Salonika was restored to Boniface, and the territory was divided up among the Crusaders. (Villehardouin's nephew Geoffrey won much of Morea, and the marshal himself was given charge of Demotika.)

Mourzuphles was captured and forced to jump from a column in Constantinople. Alexius and his wife were imprisoned. John of Wallachia was a serious threat to the new empire, and brought defeat to the Crusaders at the disastrous Battle of Adrianople. Remnants of Baldwin's army were rescued by the doge (the emperor himself had been captured). John gained control of the territory as far as Constantinople whence the Crusaders had retreated. During the following months the Crusaders attempted to hold back the ravages of John's invasions, and to maintain their few strongholds. Baldwin's brother was crowned emperor. After many battles the Crusaders managed to remake the problematic truce with another enemy, Theodore Lascaris. Boniface (Villehardouin's overlord) did homage to the new emperor, Henry. Boniface was killed in a battle against the Bulgarians in 1207.

Bibliography

(No works cited treat truth guarantees as such, however the following titles provided valuable information for the present study.)

Adams, Alison and T.D. Hemming, « *Chèvrefeuille* and the Evolution of the Tristan Legend », *Bibliographical Bulletin of the International Arthurian Society* XXVIII (1976), 204-13.

Ahlström, Axel, *Marie de France et les lais narratifs* (Gothenburg, 1925).

Alberti Aquensis Historia Hierosolymitana, Recueil des historiens des Croisades: Historiens occidentaux IV (Paris, 1879).

Alphandéry, P. and A. Dupront, *La Chrétienté et l'idée de croisade*, 2 vols. (Paris, 1954-9).

Ambroise, *L'Estoire de la Guerre Sainte*, ed. G. Paris (Paris, 1954).

Anglo-Saxon Chronicle, a revised translation, eds. D. Whitelock, D.C. Douglas, S.I. Tucker (London, 1961).

Anna Comnena, *Anne Comnène Alexiade : Règne de l'empereur Alexis I Comnène (1081-1118)*, ed. and trans. Bernard Leib, 3 vols. (Paris, 1937-45).

Archambault, Paul, *Seven French Chroniclers* (Syracuse, 1974).

Aubertin, Charles, *Les Chroniqueurs français du moyen âge : Villehardouin, Joinville, Froissart, Commines* (Paris, 18?).

Baldrici Dolensis Episcopi Historia Hierosolymitana, Recueil des historiens des Croisades : Historiens occidentaux IV (Paris, 1879).

Baldwin. M.W. ed., *A History of the Crusades, I, The First Hundred Years* (Philadelphia, 1958).

Barker Ernest, *The Crusades* (London, 1923).

Bastin, E., « La Syntaxe de Villehardouin », *Rev. Instr. pub. en Belgique* XXIX (1881), 240-55 and 300-96.

Baulier, F., « Recherches sur l'ordre des mots dans les oeuvres de G. de Villehardouin, H. de Valenciennes et R. de Clari », (Diss. Paris, 1950).

Baum, Richard, *Recherches sur les oeuvres attribuées à Marie de France* (Heidelberg, 1968).

116

Bédier, Joseph, «Les *Lais* de Marie de France», *Revue des Deux Monde* CVII (Sept.-Oct. 1891), 835-63.

Beer, Jeanette M.A., « Author-Formulae and the Differentiation o Material in Villehardouin's *La Conquête de Constantinople* » *Romance Philology* XXXII, 3 (Feb. 1979), 298-302.

— *A Medieval Caesar* (Geneva, 1976).

— « Villehardouin and the Oral Narrative », *Studies in Philolog* LXVII, 267-77.

— *Villehardouin — Epic Historian* (Geneva, 1968).

Benoit, *Chronique des ducs de Normandie*, ed. F. Michel (Paris, 1836-43)

Bolgar, R.R., *The Classical Heritage and its Beneficiaries* (Cambridge 1954).

Bonizo, *Liber de vita christiana*, ed. E. Perels, vol. I (Berlin, 1930)

Bossuat, Robert, *Manuel bibliographique de la littérature française d* *moyen âge* (Melun, 1951).

— « Traductions françaises des *Commentaires* de César à la fin du XV siècle », *Bibliothèque d'humanisme et Renaissance* III (1943) 253-411.

Bréhier, L., *L'Eglise et l'orient au moyen âge : les croisades*, 6th ed. (Paris, 1928).

— *Vie et mort de Byzance* (Paris, 1949).

— *Les Institutions de l'empire byzantin* (Paris, 1949).

— *La Civilisation byzantine* (Paris, 1950).

Brightenback, Kristine, « Remarks on the *Prologue* to Marie de France' *Lais* », *Romance Philology* XXX (1976-7), 168-77.

Bruce, James D., *The Evolution of Arthurian Romance from the Begin* *nings down to the Year 1300*, 2 vols. (Baltimore, 1928).

Brugger, Ernst, « Uber die Bedeutung von *Bretagne, breton* in mittelalter lichen Texten », *Zeitschrift für französische Sprache und Literatu* XX (1898), 79-162.

— « Eigennamen in den *Lais* der Marie de France », *Zeitschrift für fran* zösische Sprache und Literatur LXI (1927), 201-52, 381-484.

Caesar, Julius, *Bellum Gallicum* (Leipzig, 1968).

Cahen, C., *La Syrie du nord à l'époque des Croisades* (Paris, 1940).

Catalogue des actes d'Henri I, roi de France, ed. F. Soehnée (Paris, 1907)

Chalandon, F., *Essai sur le règne d'Alexis Comnène* (Paris, 1900).

Chanson d'Antioche, ed. Paulin Paris (Paris, 1848).

Chaurand, Jacques, « La Conception de l'histoire de Guibert de Noger (1053-1124) », *Cahiers de civilisation médiévale* VIII (1965), 381-96

Chroniques anglo-normandes, ed. F. Michel (Rouen, 1836-40).

Clédat, Léon, « Les *Lais* de Marie de France », *Histoire de la langue et de la littérature française des origines à 1900*, ed. L. Petit de Juleville, vol. I, pp. 285-302.

Curtius, E.R., *Europaïsche Literatur und lateinisches Mitelalter* (Bern, 1948).

— « Zur Literarästhetik des Mittelalters II », *Zeitschrift für romanische Philologie* LVIII (1938), 129-232.

Delbouille, Maurice, « Ceo fu la summe de l'escrit ...(*Chievrefoil*, 61 ss) », *Mélanges de langue et de littérature du moyen âge et de la Renaissance offerts à Jean Frappier par ses collègues, ses élèves et ses amis* (Geneva, 1970).

Delisle, L., « Liste des compagnons de Guillaume le Conquérant à la conquête de l'Angleterre en 1066 », *Bulletin monumental* XXVII (1862), 474-80.

Dembowski, P.F., *La Chronique de Robert de Clari* (Toronto, 1963).

Donovan, Mortimer J., *The Breton Lay : A Guide to Varieties* (Indiana, 1969).

Douglas, D.C., *The Norman Conquest and British Historians* (Glasgow, 1946).

— *William the Conqueror* (Berkeley and Los Angeles, 1964).

Dufournet, J., « La Bataille d'Adrianople dans la Chronique de Ville-hardouin », *L'Information littéraire* XXV, 81-92.

— «Villehardouin et Clari, juges de Boniface de Montferrat», *Revue des langues romanes* LXXIX (1969), 29-58.

— «Villehardouin et les Vénitiens», *L'Information littéraire* XXI, 7-19.

— *Villehardouin et Clari* (Paris, 1973).

Eichelberg, W., *Dichtung und Wahrheit in Machauts « Voir Dit »* (Frankfurt am Main, 1935)

Ekkehardi Uraugiensis Hierosolymita, Recueil des historiens des Croisades : Historiens occidentaux V (Paris, 1895).

Encomium Emmae reginae, ed. A. Campbell (London, 1949).

Erdmann, C., *Die Enstehung des Kreuzzugsgedankens* (Stuttgart, 1935).

Extraits des chroniqueurs français, eds. G. Paris and A. Jeanroy, 12th ed. (Paris, 1927).

Faral, E., *Les Arts poétiques du XIIe et du XIIIe siècle* (Paris, 1924).

— « Pour l'établissement du texte de Villehardouin : manuscrits conser-vés et manuscrits perdus », *Romania* LXV (1939), 204-17.

— « Villehardouin : la question de sa sincérité », *Revue historique* CLXXVII (1936), 530-582.

Fet des Romains, les, ed. L.-F. Flutre and K. Sneyders de Vogel (Paris, 1938).

118

Flodoard, *Annales*, ed. P. Lauer (Paris, 1906).

Flutre, L.-F., *Li Fait des Romains dans les littératures française et italienn* *du XIIIe au XVIe siècle* (Paris, 1932).

— *Table des noms propres avec toutes leurs variantes figurant dans le romans du moyen âge écrits en français ou en provençal et actuellement publiés ou analysés* (Poitiers, 1962).

Foreville, R., « Aux origines de la légende épique : Les 'Gesta Guillelm ducis Normannorum et regis Anglorum' de Guillaume de Poitiers » *Moyen Age* LVI (1950), 195-219.

Foulet, L., « Marie de France et la légende du Purgatoire de Sain Patrice », *Romanische Forschungen* XXII (1908), 599-627.

Frappier, J., « Les Discours dans la Chronique de Villehardouin », *Etude romanes dédiées à Mario Roques* (Paris, 1946), 39-55.

— « Le Style de Villehardouin dans les discours de sa Chronique », *Bulletin of the John Rylands Library* XXX (Manchester, 1946), 57-70

Freeman, E.A., *The History of the Norman Conquest of Englan* (Oxford, 1867-79).

Frolow, A., « La Déviation de la 4e Croisade vers Constantinople », *Revu historique des religions* CXLV, 168-187 and CXLVI, 67-89 an 194-219.

Fulcherii Carnotensis Gesta Francorum Iherusalem peregrinantium Recueil des historiens des Croisades — Historiens occidentaux II (Paris, 1866).

Gaimar, G., *L'Estoire des Engleis*, ed. A. Bell (Oxford, 1960).

Gelzer, M., *Caesar, der Politiker und Staatsmann* (Munich, 1941).

Geoffrey of Monmouth, *Historia Regum Britanniae*, ed. A. Griscom (London, 1929).

Gesta Francorum et aliorum Hierosolimitanorum, ed. J. Bongars (Hanover, 1611).

— ed. L. Bréhier (Paris, 1924).

— ed. H. Hagenmayer (Heidelberg, 1890).

— ed. R. Hill (Edinburgh, 1962).

— ed. P. Le Bas, *Recueil des historiens des Croisades : Historien occidentaux* III (Paris, 1866).

— ed. B. Lees (Oxford, 1924).

Goldschmidt, A., *An Early Manuscript of the Aesop Fables of Avianu and Related Manuscripts* (Princeton, 1947).

Gougenheim, G., « Notes sur le vocabulaire de Clari et de Villehardouin » *Romania* LXVIII (1944-5), 401-21.

Graf, Arturo, *Roma nella memoria e nelle immaginazione del medio evo* 2 vols. (Turin, 1882).

Grandes Chroniques de France, les, vol. I (Paris, 1920).

Green, J.R., *Conquest of England* (London, 1833).

Grégoire, H., « The Question of the Diversion of the Fourth Crusade », *Byzantion* XV (1941), 158-66.

Greving, B., « Studien über die Nebensätze bei Villehardouin », (Diss. Kiel, 1903).

Grousset, R., *Histoire des croisades*, 3 vols. (Paris, 1934-6).

Guibert de Nogent, *Gesta Dei per Francos, Patrologia Latina* CLVI, ed. J.P. Migne (Paris, 1880).

— *Historia quae dicitur Gesta Dei per Francos, Recueil des historiens des Croisades : Historiens occidentaux* IV (Paris, 1879).

Guillaume de Jumièges, *Gesta Normannorum ducum*, ed. J. Marx (Rouen and Paris, 1914).

Guillaume de Machaut, *Guillaume de Machaut : Poésies lyriques*, ed. V. Chichmaref, 2 vols. (Paris, 1909).

— *Le Livre du Voir-Dit*, ed. P. Paris (Paris, 1875 and rep. Geneva, 1969).

— *Les Oeuvres de Guillaume de Machaut*, ed. P. Tarbé (Paris-Reims, 1849).

— *Poésies d'Agnès de Navarre-Champagne, dame de Foix*, ed. P. Tarbé (Paris-Reims, 1856).

Guillaume de Malmesbury, *Gesta pontificum Anglorum*, ed. N.E.S.A. Hamilton (London, 1870).

— *Gesta regum Anglorum*, ed. W. Stubbs (London, 1887-1889).

Guillaume de Poitiers, *Gesta Guillelmi ducis Normannorum et regis Anglorum*, ed. R. Foreville (Paris, 1952).

Guillelmi Tyrensis archiepiscopi Historia rerum in partibus transmarinis gestarum, Recueil des historiens des Croisades : Historiens occidentaux I (Paris, 1844).

Gutsch, M.R., « A Twelfth-Century Preacher — Fulk of Neuilly », *The Crusades*, ed. L.J. Paetow (New York, 1928).

Haase, A., *Syntaktische Untersuchungen zu Villehardouin und Joinville* (Oppeln, 1844).

Hagmann, J.G., «Geoffroi de Villehardouin, sein Werk und seine Thaten», *Pages d'histoire dédiées à Pierre Vaucher* (1894), pp. 243-80.

Halphen, L., *Le comté d'Anjou au XIe siècle* (Paris, 1906).

— *Mélanges d'histoire dédiées à L. Halphen* (Paris, 1915).

Hanf, Georg, « Ueber Guillaume de Machauts Voir Dit », *Zeitschrift für romanische Philologie* XXII (1898), 145-96.

Hardy, T.H., *Descriptive Catalogue of Material Relating to the History of Great Britain and Ireland* (Rolls Series, 1862-71).

Haskins, C.H., *Norman Institutions* (Cambridge, 1918).

Henri de Valenciennes, *Histoire de l'Empereur Henri de Constantinople* (Paris, 1948).

Hervieux, L., *Les Fabulistes latins, depuis le siècle d'Auguste jusqu'à la fin du moyen âge*, 2 vols. (Paris, 1884) and 2nd. ed., 5 vols. (Paris, 1883-9).

Heyd, W. von, *Histoire du commerce du Levant au moyen âge*, trans. F. Raynaud (Leipzig, 1879, 1885, rep. 1936).

Historiae Anglicanae Scriptores, ed. R. Twysden (London, 1652).

Historia Augusta, ed. E. Hohl, 5th ed. (Leipzig, 1971).

Historia Normannorum Scriptores antiqui, ed. A. Duchesne (Paris, 1619).

Hoepffner, E., « The Breton *Lais* », *Arthurian Literature in the Middle Ages: A Collaborative History*, ed. R. Loomis (Oxford, 1959).

— « La Géographie et l'histoire dans les *Lais* de Marie de France », *Romania* LVI (1930), 1-32.

Hofer, Stefan, « Der *Tristanroman* und der *Lai du Chievrefueil* der Marie de France », *Zeitschrift für romanische Philologie* LXIX (1953), 129-31.

Hollister, C.W., *Anglo-Saxon Military Institutions* (Oxford, 1962).

Innocent III, *Correspondence, Patrologia Latina* CCXIV-CCXVII, ed. J.P. Migne (Paris, 1862).

Iorga, N., *Histoire des Croisades* (Paris, 1924).

Isidore of Seville, *Etymologiarum sive Originum*, ed. W.M. Lindsay (Oxford, 1911).

Jaquot, J.A., « Etude de Geoffroy de Villehardouin, dit le Chroniqueur et sur les Villehardouin princes d'Achaïe », *Mem. Soc. Acad. de l'Aube* XXXIII (1869), 5-56.

Körting, G., *Wilhelm von Poitiers Gesta Guilelmi ducis Normannorum et regis Anglorum* (Dresden, 1875).

Kressner, A., «Über den epischen Charakter der Sprache Villehardouins», *Archiv für neuere Sprachen* LVII (1877), 1-16.

Krey, A.C., «The Making of an Historian in the Middle Ages», *Speculum* XVI (1941), 149 ff.

— « Urban's Crusade — Success or Failure », *American Historical Review* LIII (1948), 235-50.

Larmat, J., « Sur quelques aspects de la religion chrétienne dans les Chroniques de Villehardouin et de Clari », *Moyen Age* LXXX (1974), 403-27.

Lefèvre, Y., « La Traduction du latin par un clerc français au XIIIe siècle », *Atti dell'VIII Congresso internazionale di studi romanzi* (Florence, 1959), 219 ff.

Longnon, J., *Les Compagnons de Villehardouin : recherches sur les Croisés de la quatrième Croisade* (Geneva-Paris, 1978).

— *Recherches sur la vie de Geoffrey de Villehardouin, suivies du Catalogue des actes de Villehardouin* (Paris, 1939).

Lucan, M. Annaeus, ed. and trans. J.E. Duff (London, 1928).

Lucas, R.H.,« Mediaeval French Translations of the French Classics to 1500 », *Speculum* XLV (1970), 225-53.

Machabey, A., *Guillaume de Machaut, 130?-1377 : La Vie et l'oeuvre musicale*, 2 vols. (Paris, 1955).

McNeal, E.H., « Chronicle and Conte : A Note on Narrative Style in Geoffroy of Villehardouin and Robert de Clari », *Festschrift für M. Blakemore Evans* (Columbus, 1945).

Manitius, M., *Geschichte des lateinischen Literatur des Mittelalters*, (Munich, 1911).

Marie de France, *Espurgatoire Seint Patriz*, ed. T.A. Jenkins (Philadelphia, 1894, rep. Geneva, 1974).

— *The Espurgatoire Seint Patriz of Marie de France* (Chicago, 1903).

— *Das Buch vom Espurgatoire S. Patrice der Marie de France und seine Quelle* (Halle, 1938).

— *Fables*, ed. A. Ewert and R.C. Johnston (Oxford, 1942).

— *Die Fabeln der Marie de France*, ed. Karl Warnke (Halle, 1898, rep. Geneva, 1974).

— *Lais*, ed. A. Ewert (Oxford, 1944).

— *Les Lais*, ed. E. Hoepffner, 2 vols. (Strasbourg, 1921).

— *Les Lais de Marie de France*, ed. J. Rychner (Paris, 1966).

Marx, J., « Guillaume de Poitiers et Guillaume de Jumièges », *Mélanges d'histoire offerts à F. Lot* (Paris, 1925).

Masson, P., « Eléments d'une bibliographie française de la Syrie », *Congrès français de la Syrie I* (Paris-Marseille, 1919).

Molinier, A., *Les Sources de l'histoire de France*, 6 vols. (Paris, 1901-1906).

Monfrin, Jacques, « Les Traducteurs et leur public en France au moyen âge », *L'Humanisme médiéval dans les littératures romanes du XIIe au XIVe siècle* (Paris), 247-62.

Monro, D.C., « The Speech of Pope Urban at Clermont, 1095 », *American Historical Review*, 1906.

Morris, C., « Geoffroy de Villehardouin and the Conquest of Constantinople », *History* LIII (1968), 24-34.

Morrisson, C., *Les Croisades* (Paris, 1969).

Oman, Sir C., *A History of the Art of War*, 2 vols. (London, 1924).

Ordericus Vitalis, *Historia Ecclesiastica*, ed. A. Le Prevost and L. Delisle, 5 vols. (Paris, 1838-55).

Paetow, L.J., ed., *The Crusades and other Historical Essays presented to Dana C. Munro* (New York, 1928).

Parodi, E.G., *Le Storie di Cesare nella lettaratura italiana dei primi secoli, Studi di Filologia Romanza*, vol. 2.

Pauphilet, A., « Sur Robert de Clari », *Romania* LVII (1931), 281-311.

— « Villehardouin, Robert de Clari et la conquête de Constantinople », article rep. as chapt. VII of *Le Legs du moyen âge* (Melun, 1950).

Payen, J.-C., *Le lai narratif* (Turnhout, 1975).

Perroy, E., *Les Croisades et l'Orient latin* (Paris, 1967).

Petrus Comestor, *Historia Scholastica, Das Buch der Maccabaer in Mitteldeutscher Bearbeitung* (Tübingen, 1904).

Planché, J.R., *Guillaume le Conquérant. Légende et histoire. Le chef d'armée et l'organisateur. Essai suivi d'une liste des compagnons de Guillaume* (Caen, 1927).

Poirion, D., *Le poète et le prince : l'évolution du lyrisme courtois de Guillaume de Machaut à Charles d'Orléans* (Paris, 1965).

Prescott, H.F.M., *Jerusalem Journey* (London, 1954).

Queller, D.E., *The Fourth Crusade* (Pennsylvania, 1977).

— Compton, T.K., and Campbell, D.A., « The Fourth Crusade : the Neglected Majority », *Speculum* XLIX (1974), 441-65.

Quintilian, M.F., *Institutio Oratoria*, ed. and trans. H.E. Butler (London, 1921).

Raimund of Agiles, *Historia Francorum, Recueil des historiens des Croisades : Historiens occidentaux* III (Paris, 1866).

Rambaud, M., *L'Art de la déformation historique dans les Commentaires de Cesar* (Paris, 1953).

Raynaud de Lage, G., « La Morale de l'histoire », *Le Moyen Age* LXIX (1963), 365-9.

— « Les 'romans antiques' dans l'histoire ancienne jusqu'à César », *Le Moyen Age* LXIII (1957), 267-309.

Recueil des actes des ducs de Normandie de 911 à 1066, ed. M. Fauroux (Société des Antiquaires de Normandie, 1961).

Regesta Regum Anglo-Normannorum, I, ed. H.W.C. Davis (Oxford, 1913) and II, ed. C. Johnson and H.A. Cronne (Oxford, 1956).

Riant, P., « Le Changement de direction de la quatrième croisade », *Revue des questions historiques* XXIII (1878), 71-114.

— « Inventaire des matériaux rassemblés par les Bénédictins au XVIIIe siècle pour la publication des *Historiens des croisades* », *Archives de l'Orient latin* II, 105-30.

Richard, J., *Le Royaume latin de Jérusalem*, ed. C. Hippeau (Paris, 1868).

Rickard, P., *Britain in Medieval French Literature* (Cambridge, 1956).

Ringger, Kurt, *Die Lais : zur Struktur der dichterischen Einbildungskraft der Marie de France* (Tübingen, 1973).

Ritchie, R.L.G., *The Normans in England before Edward the Confessor* (Exeter, 1948).

Robert de Clari, *La Conquête de Constantinople*, ed. P. Lauer (Paris, 1924).

Roberti Remensis Monachi Historia Hierosolymitana, Recueil des historiens des Croisades : Historiens occidentaux III (Paris, 1866).

Röhricht, R., *Geschichte des ersten Kreuzzuges* (Innsbruck, 1901).

— *Geschichte des Königreichs Jerusalem (1100-1291)* (Innsbruck, 1898).

Runciman, S., *A History of the Crusades*, 3 vols. (Cambridge, 1951-4).

Saewulf, *Relatio de peregrinatione ad Hierosolymam et Terram S. annis 1102 et 1103, Recueil de voyages et de mémoires publiés par la Soc. de Géographie* IV (Paris, 1839), pp. 818 ff.

Sallust, *Catilina* (Leipzig, 1968).

Sayous, E., « Geoffroy de Villehardouin : du caractère moral de sa Chronique », *Séances et travaux de l'Académie des sciences morales et politiques* CXXV (1886), 332-42.

Schoepperle, Gertrude, « Chievrefoil », *Romania* XXXVIII (1909), 196-218.

Schon, P.M., *Studien zum Stil des frühen französischen Prosa (Robert de Clari, Geoffroy de Villehardouin, Henri de Valenciennes)* (Frankfurt, 1960).

Scriptores rerum gestarum Willelmi Conquestoris, ed. J.A. Giles (London, 1845).

Smail, R.C., *Crusading Warfare, 1097-1193* (Cambridge, 1956).

Sneyders de Vogel, K., « Les Vers dans les Faits des Romains », *Mélanges de philologie offerts à J.J. Salverda de Grave* (Groningen, 1933).

Stenton, F.M., *Anglo-Saxon England* (Oxford, 1943).

— *William the Conqueror and the Role of the Normans* (London, 1908).

Stillwell, G., « Analogues to Chaucer's *Manciple's Tale* in the *Ovide Moralisé* and Machaut's *Voir-Dit* », *Philological Quarterly* XIX (1940), 133-8.

Strayer, J.R., « The Political Crusades of the Thirteenth Century », *History of the Crusades*, ed. K.M. Setton, vol. II, pp. 377-428.

Stubbs, W., *The Constitutional History of England*, 3 vols. (many editions).

Suchier, H., « Das Anagramm in Machauts Voir Dit », *Zeitschrift für romanische Philologie* XXI (1897), 541-5.

Suetonius, *Vitae Caesarum* I (Leipzig, 1968).

Sybel, H. von, *Geschichte des ersten Kreuzzugs*, 2nd. ed. (Leipzig, 1881).

Taylor, L.R., *Party Politics in the Age of Caesar* (Berkeley, 1949).

Thatcher, O.J., « Critical Work on the Latin Sources of the First Crusade », *Annual Report of the American Historical Association for the Year 1900 I*, 501-9, (Washington D.C., 1901).

Thomas, A., « Guillaume de Machaut et l'Ovide moralisé », *Romania* XL (1912), 382-400.

Thompson, J.W., « The Latin Historians of the Crusades », *A History of Historical Writing* I, 310-23 (New York, 1942).

Tudebodi sacerdotis Sivracencis Historia de Hierosolymitano itinere, Recueil des historiens des Croisades : Historiens occidentaux III (Paris, 1866).

Villehardouin, G. de, *La Conquête de Constantinople*, ed. J. Dufournet (Paris, 1969).

— *La Conquête de Constantinople, ed. E. Faral, 2nd. ed. (Paris, 1961).*

— *La Conquête de Constantinople, ed. N. de Wailly, revised ed. (Paris, 1882).*

Vita Haroldi (London, 1885).

Wace, *Roman de Rou et des ducs de Normandie*, ed. H. Andresen, 2 vols. (Heilbrunn, 1877).

Williman, Joseph P., « The Sources and Composition of Marie's Tristan Episode », *Studies in Honor of Tatiana Fotitch* (Washington, 1972).

Wolff, T., *Die Bauernkreuzzüge* (Tübingen, 1891).

Wolff, R.L., « The Latin Empire of Constantinople », *A History of the Crusades* II, ed. K.M. Setton, pp. 187-233.

Index

Table of contents

Composition du texte:
René Perrin – Notre-Dame 22 – CH-2013 Colombier

Impression:
Imprimerie Ch. Cavin SA – CH-1422 Grandson

Novembre 1981

Composition du texte

[illegible]erie Perrin — Notre Dame [illegible] — CH 20[illegible] Colombier

Impression

Imprimerie [illegible] Cavin SA — CH 1422 Grandson

Novembre 19[illegible]